NO
PLUS
ONE

WHAT TO DO WHEN LIFE ISN'T
A ROMANTIC COMEDY

STEPH YOUNG & JILL DICKMAN

*Names and identifying characteristics have
been (mostly) changed.*

DEDICATION:

TO SINGLE PEOPLE—

THIS ONE'S FOR YOU.

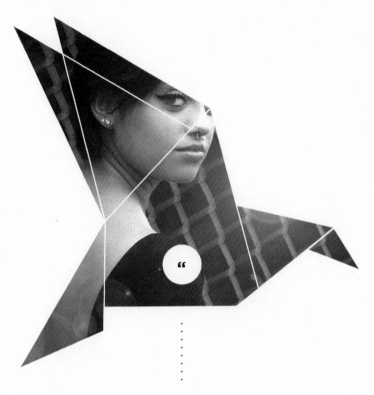

IT IS SO LIBERATING TO REALLY KNOW

WHAT I WANT, WHAT TRULY MAKES ME

HAPPY, WHAT I WILL NOT TOLERATE.

I HAVE LEARNED THAT IT IS NO ONE

ELSE'S JOB TO TAKE CARE OF ME BUT ME.

-BEYONCÉ

····· CONTENTS ·····

······ INTRODUCTION ······

don't know where it started; perhaps with Cinderella or Sleeping Beauty—sometime at a young age, I learned that finding my one true love would lead to happily ever after—end of story. Under this misguided notion, I searched for the one who would bring me my happy ending and was left feeling incomplete and inadequate when it never turned out as I had hoped.

It seemed unfair that some of my girlfriends were single for only a few tearful, teddy bear clutching days in seventh grade and I, on the other had, was encroaching on a decade of singledom. While I tried to not let my ego get battered because I had now been single for longer than I had hoped, I started to feel incredibly distraught at always being 'the single girl.' It wasn't that I hated being single, it was that I felt I had no choice. I wasn't in control of a situation, where in every other area of my life, if I put effort toward it, I could reach my goal. But finding a compatible match didn't always correlate with how many dates I went on and even if the rest of my life was taking off, my love life remained painfully stagnant. I read a million dating books and mastered every game in existence in an effort to find a man and make him my own. My friends tried to offer solutions and provided a smattering of advice such as, "You're definitely going for the wrong type of guy." "Stop being so picky." "You'll learn to love somebody." "Don't look for him and then he'll show up." After repeatedly missing the mark, I realized that a simple fairy tale formula seemed about as realistic as, well, a fairy tale. Perhaps there was more to life than finding "The One." It dawned on me that while I was pining away for a partner and beating myself up for being single, I was missing out on another life right in front of me—a single life full of autonomy, self-discovery, adventure and indulgence.

I began to look at life differently and saw that the ingredients to living a fantastic single life were there all along. I scooped these up and assembled them into the nine fundamental lessons for living life fully as a single woman. These stories and lessons allowed me start looking at my single life with a renewed sense of excitement.

01

Chapter One

ALLOW ME
TO INTRODUCE
MYSELF

AND EVERYTHING I THOUGHT I KNEW

have a friend who is a dating chameleon. She is a serial monogamist who hops quickly from one long term rela-tionship to the next without so much as a mouth-watering one night stand in between. From her high school boyfriend to her latest live-in man, she is always coupled up and in a chameleon-like way, she takes on the traits of whomever she is dating at the time. When she became a staunch vegan I took her to a trendy new vegan restaurant for her birthday dinner and was highly confused when she showed up wearing leather shoes that she'd received from her boyfriend. I found humor in this ironic scenario, but was also a little shocked at how much the influence of another person could distort her behavior.

As I reflected on this situation, I recognized that my friend wasn't the only one who seemed to struggle with knowing herself; I recognized that anytime I was under the influence of something or someone else—parents, boyfriends, religion, four shots of tequila—it was harder to know what I truly stood for and furthermore, to stand for it.

To find my happily ever after, I would first need to identify what exactly it was I wanted, be it adventure, luxury, comfort, family, excitement or perhaps a little bit of everything. Once I had a strong grasp on what I did and didn't like, it would be much easier to embark on a path to true satisfaction. Though it seems like knowing myself should've been a simple thing, I came across situations where my identity, as I had known it, was challenged. Breakups, big moves, changes in friends, and basically any time I was alone, I was forced to face myself.

I am a very, very opinionated woman, but I wasn't always this way. I became so by revisiting what I knew as a child in order to become who I was meant to be as an adult. I was raised in the Mormon religion, which is known for being extremely strict—like the no Rated-R movies, no spaghetti strap tank tops, no caffeine kind of strict. My parents, devout Mormons, had unrelenting opinions about everything; first and foremost was how our religion was the be-all-end-all to our family's life—and I went along with them. As one might imagine, I had a very sheltered upbringing, which I didn't notice until I turned 18 and struck out into the world on my own.

As I approached uncharted territory, what I realized was that I didn't have my own opinions about much of anything. I just regurgitated what I'd been taught and what I'd grown up believing because that's what my parents believed. The first time I noticed this was when I rebelliously watched an R-Rated movie. I grew up thinking anything beyond a PG rating was morally wrong. And as I watched the movie, I feared that the sky was going to fall and my parents would be the ones who had caused it. However, about 30 minutes in, the story swept me away and forgot I all about any nefarious rating. By the end I started to wonder why a Rated-R movie was off limits. I didn't feel like a bad person after watching it, and I wasn't now suddenly corrupted. Instead, I felt rather exhilarated and quite enlightened. This one moment of realization unlocked the door to exploring an entirely new belief system.

What I had never questioned growing up was now staring me back in the face and what started with an R-Rated movie seeped into many of my hard wired ideals. The thought that perhaps the Mormon religion wasn't for me started to take over. I still felt the pull of loyalty to my parents, but my own disconnected feelings toward the Mormon religion filled me with doubt. On one hand, I believed that my parents did indeed know what was best for my life; who was I to question them? On the other hand, I struggled with guilt about not inherently having the devout faith that I should. I questioned my own intuition. I questioned my normalcy. I questioned my planned future to be married and raising a family by 23. My world as I knew it was essentially unraveling when confronted with the ultimate question: was I Mormon? The answer to it would be big. It would dictate my behavior, my relationships with family, my path in life, my career goals, my friends—every piece of the puzzle that made me who I was. In short, it would dictate my identity. I was curious about every lifestyle choice that had previously been forbidden—premarital sex, caffeine, alcohol—all were beyond a line I was tempted to cross. But even so, I wasn't sure if I was ready to embark on this whole new life.

Since I hadn't felt bad watching an R-Rated movie, I wondered what else I would change my mind on and I started to explore these no-nos. First up. Sex. I had always been flirtatious as a teen, and in high school I pretty much made out with whomever I wanted and I never felt promiscuous about it. Making out was really fun, especially when there was chemistry. It also served as a stellar way to fill the time during a boring movie. But the first time I approached sex, I did so with trepidation, fully expecting to feel like a trampy little trollop who was going straight to Hell. Imagine my surprise when the self-loathing never came. After years of chaste dry humping, my first sexual experience cemented within me my opinion on premarital sex. Did I feel immoral? No. And while I didn't run out to have sex with any cute co-ed walking past my dorm room just then, I realized I had a sexual appetite and that I was not ashamed of it. This was, indeed, a defining moment.

How I felt about my own personal political views and important issues like marriage equality, despite my parents' outlook would all come in time, as I started to revisit my old beliefs with a new perspective. Though I was becoming a solid woman with strong opinions outside of what I grew up in, I still struggled to make the leap into a new life. As I wrestled with the final decision of whether or not I wanted to be Mormon, I thought of my grandfather, who wasn't Mormon but was one of the kindest men I've ever known. I was in high school when he passed away and according to the tenets of the religion in which I was raised, it was believed that he wouldn't get to rest in the highest Heaven with God. As I weighed that in my mind—that somebody I loved, who was a remarkable person—couldn't be fully honored in his passing, the scales tipped and I broke away from my childhood religion and identity completely. It was confusing at times and scary in others, but it ultimately felt freeing now that I had a new, non-Mormon world to discover.

With this new phase of life now in full swing, I wanted to continue developing my own opinions. This may sound quaint to those who never grew up in a strict religious household, but the rush I got from having a strong point of view was exhilarating and I was becoming a stronger woman in the process. And the stronger I felt, the more confident I was to go after what I wanted. By identifying even the smallest thing, like if I enjoyed watching baseball (I didn't), I became clearer and more certain about who I was. So rather than feeling forced to tolerate hours of baseball on TV while hanging out with my baseball fanatic friends, the confident, assured me could simply say, "No thanks, call me when it's over." The million small, un-groundbreaking stances I took added up. But while not liking baseball didn't have a huge impact on my day-to-day life, the overall confidence I gained while asserting myself was life changing. These defining points of view started to crystallize into a clear picture of who I was as a woman.

I continued to follow the formula I'd created and started to appraise everything I thought knew about myself. The big question became: If anything were possible, and nothing held me back—whether it be guilt, parents, money, relationships—would I still do everything exactly the same way? Big subjects, small subjects—they were all significant and would continually emerge as I got older and as my priorities changed. This is the reason getting to know myself was, and still is important. Having a strong point of view and conviction in my own identity was becoming essential to living life to the fullest. Life was easier when buoyed with confidence and self-assuredness and I was less likely to question my instincts or regret the choices I made.

Though I seemed to have everything newly figured out, I still felt unsettled and underdeveloped. Because of my naivety growing up in a sheltered environment, I knew in my heart that there was more to discover about both the world and myself. This longing led me to my first big cross country move to a small city in the south. Through a college exchange, I spent three enlightening months uncovering new territory. I imagined everything outside my small hometown to feel like a big city in comparison, and had lofty visions of living in the fast lane while enjoying a cosmopolitan lifestyle. In reality, I spent most of my time on campus; the framework of my life was defined by class, studying, working out, cheer practice and then more studying until I decided to pack it in for the night. Why so much studying? Well, besides being the super overachiever that I was (and still am), I had no friends. I belonged to the cheer squad, but mostly I was an outsider, and spent endless hours in the cafeteria at a table with my books. Sometimes people would nod hello—most of the time not. But I sat there so consistently that one day the most adorable guy, wearing a sunshine yellow T-shirt, came up to me and said, "You must have a 4.0 because you are always in here studying." That was the beginning of a meaningful and lasting friendship, and once the yellow-shirt-guy befriended me, others did too. My circle started to expand beyond my cheer team as I made friends with other lunchroom patrons. Being known as 'the girl who's always in the cafeteria' worked to my advantage, and more and more people were curious enough to swing by and meet me. Perhaps waiting for people to approach me was a lazy way to make friends—all I did was sit at a table—but it was really effective, so I put the tactic in my tool belt for future situations.

Spending so much time in the cafeteria also served another purpose; I became an avid observer of southern culture. My first observation was that grits were a main staple in every meal. Then I learned the "real" way to eat them mixed in with eggs. I preferred mine with butter and sugar, which immediately exposed me as a foreigner. It was the sugar that gave me away and I was quickly schooled that while butter was normal, adding sugar was weird. As I continued my crash course in southern culture, I was soon able to decipher accents formed by basically cutting every sentence, phrase and word in half. I picked up on new slang, but failed to ever authentically use "fiddna" in a conversation and kept to its non-south equivalent "going to." I realized that soul food was an entire culture of its own and observed old fashioned manners showcased by the ubiquitous use of "sir" and "ma'am." The south, it turned out, was everything but fast paced, and even though the population was bigger than the place I came from, it had a rural and hospitable vibe.

These entirely new facets of culture entertained me, but on the flip side, I was exposed to some of the more unfavorable traits of the south. Growing up in a homogenous area, I had only learned about racial tensions from history class. I thought racism was of the past, and up to that point hadn't experienced anything to give me reason to believe otherwise. However, unofficial segregation was a prominent part of this new culture I was experiencing and the innate antiquated belief system made life here anything but modern and liberal. While I was getting a kick out of my southern escapades, each one ended up leaving me with a bitter aftertaste.

Because I was part of the cheer team, we got to travel to some away games. Our team was tight and affectionate, and always had a blast cracking jokes and being silly. As I cheered in a new stadium, I got a thrill hitting stunts with my partner and performing on the sidelines. After one particular game, our cheer team bus stopped at an all you can eat buffet diner. My stunt partner and I got off the bus holding hands, but as we neared the entrance of the restaurant he dropped my hand and said, "not here." I looked at him for further clarification, and he explained that us seen holding hands, since we looked like an interracial couple, would cause a stir, and that was the type of trouble he didn't want to get into. The notion that our affection could turn out to be dangerous was both astonishing and disturbing. Unsettling situations continued to crop up. I watched a friend being ostracized from her family for dating outside her race. When checking out at even the most basic convenience store, I would see a full stock of knickknacks emblazoned with confederate flags and discriminatory phrases.

After three short months, it was obvious that this way of life wasn't history, and in fact was still very real. Though it was an adventure, this detour to the south looking for a shiny, cosmopolitan lifestyle didn't quite turn out as I had hoped. Despite missing the mark on finding a place I loved completely, I still got exactly what I was after, which was an escape from uniformity and boredom. Moving to an unknown place was the perfect way to grow, to see new things, and by process of elimination, get closer to knowing what I really wanted. It became clear that I wanted to be immersed in culture, but my definition of culture had changed. I wasn't just looking for different than my status quo, I wa-

looking for more; I wanted to be surrounded by buzzing city life, liberal open-mindedness, unique people and originality.

Aside from gaining a clear understanding of what I wanted, I learned more about who I was in those three months than I had in my lifetime thus far. It turned out I was a woman capable of taking a big risk and being on my own. I was able to make friends when I had none. I was a person who liked the challenge of venturing into the unknown and working it out. And above all, if something wasn't living up to my expectations, I learned that I was incredibly flexible and had no problem changing directions. I had found a effective way to truly learn who I was; putting myself in uncharted territory and seeing what I would make of it—where I go, who I make friends with, how I would handle adversity and the unexpected—all provided insight. The answers and outcomes of all of these things created a well-defined picture of who I was.

——— LESSON ———

Being single allows lots of time to figure out who you are; don't waste it by not exploring. Use it to become stronger and more confident; become the best version of yourself. Superhero You.

······ **HOMEWORK** ······

1. THINK ABOUT EVERYTHING YOU KNOW and believe and question yourself. Humor yourself and imagine what life would be like if you took the other path. Would you feel better, worse? Why? Look at the big issues you've been living with all your life, where you live, who you live with, who your friends are. Then look at the little things, like what you watch on TV, how you respond to people. Start to explore those parts where you feel a little twinge in your gut and follow it.

2. PICK A SUBJECT and create a strong argument that is opposite of your stance on the subject. Be as convincing as possible.

3. PICK A MONTH AND DO ONE TO TWO THINGS a week that you normally wouldn't do. Ask your friends for challenges.

02

Chapter Two

THE EX FILES

How to Get Over an Ex

njoying the freedom of being single is one of life's greatest pleasures. Feeling no pressure to consider anybody else when making all decisions is indulgently selfish and yet enjoyable. However when my mind is stuck in the past, dwelling on failed relationships and thoughts of what could have been, being single feels like torture. But as I've grown older I realized I can't enjoy the fruits of being accountable to nobody when I am prisoner to my thoughts.

There have been a few exes in my past that have taken all but an exorcism to get over. The first time I totally lost control of my mind was when I dated a boy named Seth in high school and on and off for a few years after. He would come over to my house, sit in the living room and talk to me with my toes tucked under his thigh. Sometimes he would bring his guitar and sing me songs. He wrote me poems and held my hand. Because of these moments, I can still understand why this was the first guy I fell in love with and why I was so devastated when our relationship didn't work out. I was sure we would end up together, married with a family that would dance and sing together. We'd be like the Osmonds but less weird. I imagined a stable family life that matched my Mormon upbringing. At the time, I wanted children and to be a mother. I wanted to do cute mom and wife things like cutting crusts off peanut butter and jelly sandwiches and teaching my kids the alphabet. But eventually my dreams of family bliss hit a wall when Seth turned 19. He, also Mormon, left on a two year mission and while he was away, I changed, realizing I didn't want to be a Mormon anymore. While I no longer prescribed to our family-based religion, sometimes I still imagined Seth and our would-be family life together. The Christmas sing-a-longs and easy romance Seth would've brought into my life wasn't an easy thought to let go. Throughout the years, I would be enjoying my nightly, non-Mormon glass of red wine and catch myself feeling not only nostalgic, but also sad at the thought that perhaps maybe I should've waited for Seth. There was always the perpetual curiosity, a question that terrified me more than any other: "What if he was my One?" I feared that I was now doomed to be single forever because I somehow screwed up my destiny. Logic kicked in, of course—he moved on and married the woman he obviously considers to be "The One" so that meant he probably wasn't mine, but the shadow of doubt that I could have ruined my future haunted me more often than seemed normal.

The thoughts of Seth and my lost Partridge Family future weren't incredibly hindering in my day-to-day life, but I noticed that every new potential boyfriend immediately ran the mental gauntlet of "are you as good as Seth?" Any guy who didn't play the guitar was crossed off the list and would only make it one or two dates. Any guy who didn't mention family life or the desire to have children, ended up only being a short-lived fling. I wouldn't even consider the thought of a long-term relationship with anybody that didn't identically match everything Seth was. Though I had thought I moved on from Seth, he was still attending every date I went on. I realized that if I kept comparing every potential guy to Seth and what could've been, I would be holding myself back from what could be. I had to stop thinking about the sweet memories we shared and how good it might have been. If wanted to ever get over him, I knew I had to start to rewire my brain somehow and so began my self-intervention.

In all these dreams and memories of Seth I realized I was only remembering the good stuff and totally forgetting all the reasons it didn't work out. So for an uncharacteristic moment, I not only focused on the negative, I embraced it. Instead of mourning the family musicals that never were, I made a list. I imagined the reality my life would have been had we ended up together. This "reality" started in the morning with no coffee, because I would then be Mormon, and wrapped up without my nightly glass of red wine that I loved so dearly. This would-be life involved no particular career ambitions and completely devoting my life to morals I didn't whole-heartedly believe in. I realized that a real life with Seth meant not only committing to him, but also committing to the life I left behind years ago. This more real version of what a future Mormon life looked like was enough make me realize that perhaps the idea of Seth was what I was after, not necessarily Seth himself. While the "Negative List" was helpful, I still caught little remembrances of him that would sneak into my mind in unexpected times. Instead of wallowing in nostalgia I decided to run interference and brainwash myself. I came up with a couple tactics and experimented with them over the next month. Any time I thought of him, I made up a mantra and repeated in my head: "Nobody is worth giving up red wine for." When a song came on shuffle that used to be his favorite, I immediately switched it to the newest dance hit and free-styled my heart out. I threw away his cozy hand-me-down sweatshirt I had been holding onto since high school. I blocked his posts from my social feed. It seemed taking action and going on the offensive started to kick me out of the Seth spell. I finally saw that I had created this fantasy haze from good memories that had become my fairy tale that never was; and then I realized that it was only a fantasy.

While I was finally able to move beyond Seth, I still was no stranger to heartbreak and the crippling thoughts that came with. Years later I dated Casey. We got to a point where we started living together. Because of this roommate situation, Casey and I grew extremely comfortable around each other. Though I was usually one to never leave the house without a pulled together outfit and hair and makeup done, Casey thought I was the most beautiful when I was simply, plainly, me —hair pulled back and fresh faced. He often said he preferred me in sweat pants, which was awesome because it never took longer than 20 minutes to get ready for anything. While I loved the extra time added to my life for more important things, like catching up on an entire Netflix season, it was not so great for the excitement in our relationship. While Casey and I loved playing house, and didn't mind a domesticated routine for the time being, he eventually became terrified of being tied down and bored with the "rut" we were in. He left both the relationship and our apartment with a lackluster goodbye, while me and my sweatpants were left in the rubble of our domesticated past. Casey's constant attention and ego boosts came to a screeching halt and I felt like I had lost my air supply. I mourned the passing of our would-be adorable, albeit comfortable future. I reeled at the idea that if maybe had I not gotten quite so comfortable, he would've stayed. Then I got angry with him for encouraging me to be my purest self and then leaving me for it. No matter which emotion I went through, one thing was consistent, I didn't want to show my face to the outside world because at the very root of my sadness was embarrassment. My self-worth took a nosedive after being broken up with yet again. When weeks before I felt beautiful au naturel, now I felt frumpy and ugly.

Was my comfortable cocoon really that bad of a place that somebody wouldn't want to be here with me?

After I ran through the gamut of emotions of sadness, betrayal, anger, and bitterness I finally landed on determination. I decided that, as a symbol of my newly forced singleness, I would rediscover the person that I used to enjoy so much. And even if I didn't feel beautiful and coveted that moment, I heeded the advice of my best fiend, "Fake it till you make it." She also used to say, "Look good to feel good," so I figured some combination of the advice would work like a magic potion.

I started with the essentials and pulled out my eyeliner, eyelash curler, brushes, blush, bronzer, mascara, eye shadows, and lipsticks and got to work. Once my makeup was done, I went to the back of my closet and found my favorite heels. After assembling my complete look I stood in front of the mirror and thought, "Damn, girl. Good to see you again!" I still looked like me but it was a version of me that I hadn't seen in a while. It was a small but symbolic way for me to remind myself that I was still amazing, with or without somebody telling me how amazing I was all the time; I could just as easily please myself. By revisiting the person I was comfortable being before the relationship, I was reminded that true self-confidence comes from within, not from my outfit and certainly not from my boyfriend—I was fabulous with or without a man. Once I started pulling myself together, a few things started to happen. My friends and coworkers noticed and complimented me on how great I looked post breakup. They would say things like, "You're hot! He doesn't know what he's missing."

While the surface validation was always welcome, it was more than just looking good that triggered my newfound confidence. By faking how amazing I felt all the time, and playing the part to go with it, I actually started to believe it. When I would force myself to say, "Girl, you are the fucking best!" in the mirror, I would get a tinge of energy if I said the statement enough days in a row. By playing the part of awesome ex that never gets ruffled, I actually started to do more, such as reaching out to my friends for happy hour and leaving the house to show off my newly washed and styled hair. This made me realize that domesticated or single, I was awesome and life was good. All these pieces added up—the compliments from coworkers, smiles from strangers, hours of distraction, self-love—and soon I hadn't remembered the last time if felt like a hopeless reject. I had moved on without even remembering that I should be depressed about being single again. Single wasn't looking so bad and neither was I.

It turned out, the formula of "Fake it till you make it" and "Look good to feel good" worked and would forever become part of my post-breakup repertoire. It worked so well that I adopted it pretty much anytime I was feeling down. However, even with this piece of trickery in my back pocket, I would find that I still wasn't immune to being heartbroken.

Perhaps one of the worst breakups I went through was when I dated Dylan. At the time I met him, I had been resistant to any new relationship, but we immediately hit it off and my walls of resistance crumbled quickly; it required very little effort to let down my guard. For the independent and self-sufficient woman I was, it was a surprising and welcome change to surrender to somebody else. Soon I felt comfortable thinking of Dylan as my other half. I started to feel like we were the cute couple in a romantic comedy. We laughed at inside jokes; he brought me candy and other little gifts. He was the person I would ask to help with an e-mail to my boss and any purchase over $50. We ate lunch together, worked out together, IM'd all day and Skyped when we were apart. Dylan quickly became invaluable to my everyday. Not only was he acting as my boyfriend, he ended up playing every role in my life including my best friend, my therapist, my entertainer and my advice-giver. After months of feeling more and more in love with each other, he said he wasn't ready for a real commitment and because it was too painful to think of anything but being with him, we stopped talking altogether. I felt like I had been taken for a fool. He had rocked me to sleep; lulled me into a comfortable codependent state then left me without a hint of trouble in paradise. I felt completely lost. It was hard to go from the constant all-day-long communication we had established through text, e-mail, Gchat and in person conversations to the silence without him. It was a hard truth to realize that I had become so dependent on one person for so many things; without Dylan as a part of my everyday, I felt really alone and extremely lonely. Every time I had a funny joke that only he would laugh at, it was torture to keep it to myself. When I had a bad day at work and all I wanted was a comforting hug in his familiar arms, I faced the depressing thought that I had nobody else I could call to replace him. Because I was so content with Dylan as my go to person, I had no desire to try and fill the holes he left. But finally after weeks of crying myself to sleep, I got tired of feeling like crap. With an ounce of willpower and a nudge from a close friend, I made the decision to take responsibility for my own happiness. And so I began the journey to once again become independent and find a solution for all the roles Dylan once played in my life.

My first outlet was to reach out to the friends that I had grown apart from. At first, I wasn't sure they'd want to hang out because I honestly hadn't been a great friend, plus lately, I wasn't that much fun to hang out with. But as I have learned time and time again, my girlfriends are the best other halves I could ever have. "Though thick and thin, richer or poorer" was never so relevant than it was with my girlfriends. One happy hour at a time, I reconnected with friends that I hadn't hung out with during the course of my relationship with Dylan. Even though I didn't always feel like going out to happy hour, pretending I was in a good mood and finding things besides my sadness to talk about helped me be in a better mood. My friends were always eager to have fun and soon I was swept away in our laughter and good times. Reaching out to friends also gave me the opportunity to listen to somebody else's problems and triumphs. Being there for my friends gave me a much-needed distraction from the thoughts of my ex and my own depression. Reconnecting with each one of these people was refreshing.

As we caught up about life, I was truly able to see each

friend as an individual gem who brought a unique quality to my life. One friend was passionate about nonprofit work and inspired me to be a more caring person. Another friend was purely hilarious and entertained me for hours on end. Another was ambitious, always encouraging me to be brave and go after what I truly wanted. When I looked around, I realized that what I had wanted Dylan to be so badly, I already possessed through every single person in my life.

Lastly, I rediscovered myself and focused on the person I was without him. While I was used to running my major shopping decisions past Dylan before purchase, I challenged myself to do research on the purchase and rely on my gut instead. I found I was also quite capable of getting candy for myself whenever my sweet tooth hit. Spending all this time with myself, and my closest friends, reminded me that I was smart, excellent at my job, charismatic and loving. When I was no longer tied to a relationship or dependent on Dylan, I was subsequently freed up to make the biggest career move of my life. Not relying on him to step up as my savior allowed me to become my own hero. In the end I realized that trusting myself and investing in my friends, who were consistently loyal, was more fulfilling than any relationship I had had to date.

At different points in time I've had to fight thoughts of exes like they were demons trying to take over the goodness in my life. While I definitely don't think I'm immune to heart-break, I am confident I've got the tools to help move on quickly and to not lose myself in the process.

—— **LESSON** ——

Recovery from an ex starts with taking the first step.

······ **HOMEWORK** ······

1. FOCUS ON THE NEGATIVE. Seriously, make a list of all the reasons it DIDN'T work out.

2. OUT WITH THE OLD, IN WITH THE NEW—take control. Make up a mantra that you can say every time a memory of your ex plays in your head. Get rid of old clothes and trinkets that were a testament to how awesome your relationship was (be honest, that T-shirt still smells like him and you love it). If you shared a place together, replace some furniture so the ghost of your ex still isn't cozying up to you every night when you catch up on your shows.

3. COME UP WITH A MANTRA that will remind you why exactly you don't need to be with this person.

4. THROW OUT ALL REMINDERS OF YOUR EX.

5. FAKE IT UNTIL YOU MAKE IT—the quickest way to feel better is to fake feeling better.

6. LOOK GOOD; FEEL GOOD—the fastest way out of a rut and the easiest confidence boost out of misery

is to get dressed up. Go spray tan, get a facial, hair done, mani/pedi, whatever it takes—feeling fabulous shows up as confidence and is a self-perpetuating cycle.

7. FRIENDS, FRIENDS AND MORE FRIENDS. It's nearly impossible to feel lonely with a full social calendar. Bonus when your friends are awesome and inspire you to be a better person. Double bonus if they are funny people and hook you up with a night of laughter—after all they say laughter is the best medicine.

8. GO BACK TO YOUR ROOTS. Once you take away all your crutches, you'll see that you a strong enough person to stand on your own two feet. Take off the training wheels and discover an independent woman who makes her own happiness.

03

Chapter Three

WHEN GOOD FRIENDS GIVE BAD ADVICE

BEING SINGLE CAN BE HARD.
BAD ADVICE CAN MAKE IT HARDER.

Not long ago I turned into Angry Chick. I had been on one too many bad dates and the frustration of it all started to show up in my everyday demean-

or. At any given time, when I reached my dating frustration quota, Angry Chick came on much like the incredible hulk—not as green but every bit as scary. She radiated bitterness and threw daggers with her eyes at every deserving (and undeserving) man that crossed her path. She's not a nice person, and I had become her.

I was so fed up that men weren't meeting my (already low) expectations that I ended up bitterly yelling at any commercial that dared show happy couples bonding over their shared new car excitement. How was it possible that almost everywhere I turned there were women left and right snagging boyfriends, and I couldn't even get a guy to ask me out on a date…or return a text message? Nobody liked to hang out with Angry Chick and I was convinced that the only thing that compensated for my bitterness was my entertaining stories of dating tragedy. My happily coupled friends would gasp, "Oh my God, REALLY!? That actually happened?" as I told them my horror stories, and then they would follow up with, "I'm so glad I don't have to deal with that anymore."

Yes. How nice for them.

Though I was happy to entertain my friends and be the high-light of any party with my catastrophic tales of the single life, it sucked to be a failure in a part of my life where I instead wanted to be earning gold stars. Usually the best way to deal with failure is to seek out an expert for guidance. And who better to give that guidance than somebody who had been successful at finding and maintaining a relationship?

One night, my alter ego, Angry Chick, was venting to my friend Roslyn over a glass of wine. I described my latest escapade—one that was all too familiar—in which, upon initial meeting, Paul and I had great chemistry. He seemed like a gentleman and in a night out treated me to dinner and unlimited vodka sodas. He was tall, athletic, charming and funny—not to mention so handsome that he immediately caused me to lose my train of thought and blush from head to toe upon seeing him. I told Roslyn all the adorable things he did, along with the flirtatious hand holding that led to an epic make out session on the dance floor. Then I replayed the weeks that followed that magical night. Short replies and broken plans. After one brush off too many, I finally got fed up and stopped trying to hang out with him again.

"What gives?" I asked Roslyn, who seemed to have it all figured out in the relationship world.

Roz enlightened me with, "I think you're just coming on too

strong. Guys like the chase."

While this may or may not be biologically true, I would put money down (LOTS of money) that if a poll were taken of relationships, most would credit the woman taking initiative in one way or another. Maybe she didn't outwardly ask her love interest out on a date, but she probably had a hand in their getting together. Women run the world behind the scenes and have been doing so for ages. Relationships are probably no different.

But unlike writing cover letters, folding a fitted sheet, or cooking, successful relationships didn't seem to have a formula. The fact is, seeking advice from my girlfriends and then taking that advice has often proved to be a mistake. Though I was always grateful for the unlimited hours my friends spent trying to help me solve my dating dilemmas, though well-intentioned, much of the advice I received ended up confusing me more. It started to make me feel like I was the reason I was still single. Each time I heard, "Where are you going to meet guys?" "You need to look friendlier, like maybe try smiling more and look them in the eyes," or "You should dress more/less revealing," I felt like I needed to change something about myself in order to be in a relationship or even be worthy of attracting a guy's attention.

After hearing a ton of frivolous advice, it started to feel like I was doing all the wrong things while everyone around me was pairing up and counting off relationship milestones.

This led to me looking at all the successful relationships around me and wonder "Why not me? When will it be my turn?" On multiple occasions I had blurted this out to a friend, who's in a relationship, only to hear the response, "It will happen when you aren't looking for it."

This was an intriguing concept. Although this principle may be true when applied to car keys or my favorite shirt, I had yet to hear of somebody who'd found their special someone when they weren't looking. I'd needled my way in and out of bitterness and busyness throughout my life. Occasionally I'd been broken-hearted. All of these states typically kept me from going out on dates, meeting new people, or even looking up anytime I ventured out into public. However, even during my most distant days, I never stopped hoping to find love eventually. In light of this realization, I finally started to question what this saying—you'll find it when you're not looking—really meant. I ultimately found it to be impossible. I was a person who wanted to find love, therefore no matter how bitter, busy or broken I became, because I hoped to find love, by default, I would always be looking. For instance, no matter how busy I got at work, while I might not have been going out on extra dates, I wasn't blind to how handsome my male coworkers would become after spending endless hours with them. As I was healing from a broken heart, I didn't miss that my guy friend always said and did just the right thing to console me. Even though I wasn't looking to my guy friend for dates and romance, his companionship was a quality that I recognized as a trait I was looking for.

This wasn't the only time the single girl remedies my friends imparted on me were not helpful. Though my friends' advice to find a man kept me busy, it certainly didn't bring me any success. In fact, these "remedies" were quite defeating. But after a bit of defeat, bottom line was finally starting to stick: If I failed with these "rules," I was not the failure, the "rule" was.

So with that realization, I took a stand for all single girls, and, for convenience and future reference, dispelled every piece of [bad] advice I ever received.

FAULTY ADVICE #1

"DON'T BE TOO CRAZY"

One time I started dating a guy casually, we weren't an item, but I liked him a lot. When I started to bring up little things like another girl's flirty comment on his Instagram, he would subtly brush me off and remind me we were still only in the beginning and not-so-serious stage of hanging out. As I later recounted my frustration to my friend, Karen, she was shocked that I had called him out on an Instagram comment. She warned me that if I was too open with my insecurities at this early stage in the relationship, this guy would think I was "crazy" and stop dating me.

I let that advice sink in and started to think that maybe I was being too crazy if something as small as an Instagram comment was getting under my skin. As I tried to reason with myself, I considered another friend of mine, who was so emotional and irrational she would rank pretty high on the crazy scale. She, however, made no attempt to hide any of her irrational antics, and ended up engaged. Her fiancé kept coming back even though he got kicked out of their apartment every other week. Okay, so perhaps it wasn't "the crazy" that was keeping me from a relationship.

Though I had not solved my dating dilemma with this new guy, I did feel better about being up front with my emotions.

FAULTY ADVICE #2

"YOU NEED TO RAISE YOUR STANDARDS"

I'm pretty notorious for giving almost anybody a chance. In the spirit of being open minded, I will entertain the idea of a date with all types. This in turn, has led to many dates that have made my friends cringe. After recounting yet another failed attempt with a guy who, turned out had very little ambition, my friend, Andrew, forbade me to date anybody else who didn't have a car and a full-time job. His reasoning was that if a guy wasn't ambitious enough to find a job and therefore able to afford a car, then I would run circles around him, and it wouldn't end up working out anyway. Though he had a point, I countered with the story of one of my sisters. She had been through multiple marriages. Husband number one was smoking hot, incredibly nice and of course, had a great sense of humor. When life got in the way, and their marriage didn't workout, she got back on the bandwagon and eventually found a well educated, 4th grade teacher. While he was everything on paper, smart, handsome, active, etc, their lifestyle differences ultimately led to the end of this relationship. Though my sister always had great success filling her high expectations, she wasn't finding lasting happiness.

A while later, she moved to a new state and started dating a guy who drove a beat up car, was trying to find work out of school and was 10 years her junior. Every friend and family member was screaming, "Stay away! He's too immature, he doesn't have his life together, raise your expectations." But my sister, who had seemingly learned her lesson, didn't listen to all of the naysayers. It was the happiest I'd known her to be. Ever. If she had listened to the 'raise your standards rule,' she never would've gotten to know this guy, nor have experienced the happiness she had found.

Faulty Advice #3

"YOU NEED TO LOWER YOUR STANDARDS"

During a random brainstorm with some girlfriends about why I didn't yet have a boyfriend, they all arrived at a consensus—I needed to lower my standards. This piece of advice confused me because just prior I was advised to raise my standards. Though I date a wide array of guys—tall, short, funny, nerdy, fluffy and soft, hot as hell, white, black, local, foreign and everywhere in between I often get accused of having a type. I considered my friends' advice to lower my expectations and because I had a pretty proven track record of giving a lot of guys a chance, I was a little miffed that my girlfriends would even suggest that my standards were too high. I concluded that perhaps others assume a single girl is being too picky otherwise surely we'd find somebody, right? I wasn't sure how much lower I could go with some of my dating considerations and wondered, which expectation did they think I should lower. Was it the one where a guy wants to spend time with me? Or perhaps the one where he doesn't flirt with other girls via Instagram? The conflicting advice was starting to pile up, and the less seriously I took it, the more I started to understand that there is no magic formula for dating. This, however, didn't stop anyone from providing more unsolicited advice.

FAULTY ADVICE #4

"DON'T MEET PEOPLE AT THE BAR/WORKPLACE/GYM/ETC."

After finishing up a month full of dates with guys from

Tinder, Ok Cupid, a club, a bar, a mutual friend and work, I was exhausted. I had heard from a variety of friends one version or another of the advice, "Don't meet a guy at [fill in the blank]. However, the one that is probably the most prevalent is don't meet a guy at a bar. While I generally agree that making solid potential relationship choices may not happen while incredibly intoxicated, I even questioned my own logic when I was talking to my friend, Evie. Though I'd known Evie for years, I had never asked her how she and her totally devoted husband, Joe, met. She responded with, "We met at the bar in the Red Lion Hotel." My first response was, "Ooh, classy." She then continued to tell me the most adorable story of their budding true love. That, her eight-year marriage and two adorable kids were enough to shatter this "rule" forever.

Faulty Advice #5

"DON'T HOOK UP ON THE FIRST DATE"

Sex is a part of life, or at least it should be. Being single for any long period of time lends itself to having more sexual partners than somebody who's been in a relationship for say, six years. Because of this, I don't always have the patience to go through a month's worth of dating when I'm really just in the mood to get some action. Though I don't always hook up on the first date, it's been known to happen. Sometimes a hook up led to another date, sometimes it led to nothing. Either way, I can't count how many times a friend has told me to wait.

One date I went on was a much-needed reprieve from the drought I was in at the time. A good friend had introduced me to Mike, and after a few weeks of casual text conversations, we finally met up for drinks. Immediately upon seeing Mike, I silently praised my friend for having such amazing taste—Mike was hot. We ended up hanging out for hours and having an incredibly refreshing conversation. It was nice to connect with somebody new and to feel stimulated both mentally and physically. Throughout the date I used all my self-control to not jump over the table and start making out with him. But I did start to ramp up the flirting and close in on the physical distance between us. By the end of the night, all my flirting was paying off and he stayed the night at my place…action ensued.

The next morning he left with a smile and promised to call but much to my dismay, he never did. We exchanged a few more text messages, initiated by me, but despite my enthusiasm to hang out again, he never followed through. I was really disappointed that after finally meeting somebody I was interested in, I was back to being single with no explanation on why Mike disappeared. I vented to my friend Roz and she doled another version of her guys-like-the-chase advice, only this time it sounded like, don't hook up on the first date.

In my dejected and weakened state I listened intently and started to question my previous behavior. Maybe it was true—that should wait longer to have sex so he'll be emotionally invested before I give it up. But then I remembered the 12-year marriage of my sister and her husband, who slept together on their very first date and saw that "rule" didn't hold up either.

My sister Kareen had always been a believer in the "do what you feel is best" mantra, and did exactly that with her husband of now 12 years. She met him while working at a day care; his son was her favorite. Eventually they had a child-free play date and my sister had sex with him right away because, as she put it, "I wanted to say I'd had sex with someone who was that hot." Fast forward 12 years later—it turns out her decision to act upon her urges didn't ruin her chance at being with this guy forever.

And with an ironic twist of fate, soon after Roz had given me her brilliant "you should wait" advice, she went on a business trip and hooked up with her now fiancé at a party.

Some relationships work out after sex on the first date, some don't. There seemed to be no formula. I started to realize that while my friends were trying to help, instead of avoiding forbidden date behavior, perhaps I should avoid seeking advice about how to fix my dating life.

FAULTY ADVICE #6

"GO OUT MORE TO MEET PEOPLE, LIKE AT A BAR/COFFEE SHOP/GYM/ETC."

After I surrendered to the idea that maybe there is no magic solution to landing a man, I found it entertaining how all these rules started to contradict themselves. After a particular boring phase in my single life, a friend suggested faulty advice #6 and mentioned that I should get out more. While generally I agreed with her, that Prince Charming definitely wasn't going to manifest in my living room, I countered that being out wasn't going to magically turn up a boyfriend either.

Though I had been going through a reclusive phase, I typically was out all the time. I would go to coffee shops to write, commute to work, grab happy hour with friends, workout at the gym and occasionally I'd buy groceries at a grocery store. However, I was still single. I realized that though getting out more may increase my chances of meeting new people, it wasn't the make-or-break factor in finding a relationship. But I did give this rule some credit. Though I may not end up with a boyfriend, getting out of my house has led to some really great experiences, which in turn has made single life more fun.

Faulty Advice #7

"DON'T SCARE HIM AWAY"

The last piece of faulty advice I'd received didn't come about from any particular failed attempt but rather a general observation about my apartment. My friend and I were sitting in my living room sharing a bottle of wine and gabbing away when she subtly mentioned that I should probably hide my full 8-season collection of Charmed DVD's. I paused for a second and as I looked at her with a raised eyebrow, she furthered that it wasn't the best look for when I had guys over—they might think I was weird. I thought of all the things wrong with my apartment. Sometimes it looked like WW3 aftermath. I had a sentimental stuffed animal in my bedroom. My wine glasses were all unique, some with stems, some without and some were goblets. My pantry and fridge had an abundance of condiments but the only thing of sustenance was a box of Special K, that if in a real bind I could eat dry because I never had any milk. I took in her advice but argued that if I acquiesced and hid the eight seasons of Charmed DVDs, I would feel like I would be trying to hide something that made me uniquely me. I argued if a guy couldn't accept me for everything that I am in the beginning, he most likely would not be able to handle me at any point in time. So with that I held onto my confidence and vowed to always be myself. Always.

I have found that when I followed my friends' arbitrary advice and tried to control various dating outcomes, I ultimately set myself up for failure. What I've realized is that the only thing my friends can tell me is how it worked for them. The harsh reality is that no one really knows definitively how to land a good relationship.

All I can do is stay true to what I'm feeling and trust that life will unfold as it should.

—— **L ESSON** ——

It's not good advice if it makes you feel bad about yourself. Look at each situation individually and decide what is the best course of action for you.

······ **HOMEWORK** ······

1. THE NEXT TIME SOMEBODY GIVES you advice, listen respectfully. Then start weighing out the validity and the irrationality of each suggestion. If the advice makes you feel hopeless or inadequate, try to uncover the underlying reason. Then when you are done, let it go and don't beat yourself up for being single. On the flip side, if there is a suggestion you haven't tried, throw it in your dating repertoire. If you've never waited a month before you've hooked up with somebody new, try it and see what works and what doesn't. It may still not be the perfect solution to dating woes, but it's a perfect opportunity for self-discovery.

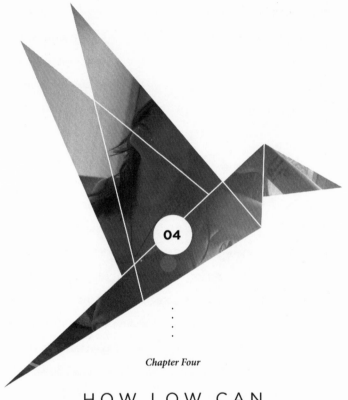

Chapter Four

HOW LOW CAN YOU GO?

KEEPING YOUR HEAD HIGH AND YOUR STANDARDS HIGHER.

The line between being single and settling is one most don't want to cross. It can be a difficult decision when faced with two terrifying options: Be single indefinitely or settle. These have felt like my only options more times than I can count. Dating someone (anyone) seemed like the much better option when faced with lonely nights pining for a man. However, I learned that settling typically led me down a slippery slope of unsatisfying connections, unfulfilled expectations, wasted time and hurt feelings.

I was single during a large majority of my college years; eventually all my friends were coupled up and I was fed up and ready for my turn. I had recently been denied by my latest crush Adam; that rejection on top of a few years of single life had me feeling like something was wrong with me. People would say things like, "You're so adorable, why are you single?" Though my typical response was just to shrug it off with a nondescript reply, deep down I feared that the answer was because nobody wanted to be my boyfriend. I was lonely and yearning to be a part of a couple; I wanted to feel special to somebody.

It was during this phase when I met Bryce at a college hangout with some mutual friends. He was abrasive and talked too much. His arrogance was a turnoff, but I was nice to him anyway. Bryce mistook my niceness as interest and started paying attention to me. Though I didn't really like him that much, the attentiveness felt like a drug. After being denied by my previous crush, Bryce fed my starved ego. It felt nice to be coveted. He came on strong, and without realizing it, I got swept up in how much he liked me.

On our first date Bryce and I walked around campus holding hands and talking at length about books and music. While he did majority of the talking, it felt nice to be playing out a little portion of my RomCom fantasies. He was enthusiastic about me and us. Over the next few weeks he would meet me between classes just to say hello. We would make out for hours, talk on the phone and go to basketball games together. Because he was always pursuing me, all I really had to do was say yes and show up. Though his personality still took a bit of grit to pallet, I convinced myself to overlook his annoying traits and keep focused on what I was after—a relationship. I liked his adoration so much that I tolerated his one-sided conversations.

We moved quickly down boyfriend/girlfriend lane and, after four weeks, we had already exchanged I love you's and met each other's parents. Bryce and I checked off relationship milestones with urgency. I was so deep into being part of a couple and had done such a thorough job of convincing myself that I was actually in love with him that I overlooked one key thing: I didn't really even like him.

One afternoon, we were hanging out in the campus gym, flirting and playing around. Bryce was trying to get me to laugh with playful nudges and tickling when I coyly said, "Stop Adam!" Maybe had I tried to cover up this Freudian slip he wouldn't have even noticed; but instead I froze like I had just been caught robbing a bank. The lie that I had even convinced myself was true was exposed in a flash. Once my old crush's name slipped out of my mouth with such adoration, Bryce and I both knew our relationship was over. Bryce was devastated and after endless breakup talks, we finally parted ways. I had been with him for two months, yet under all the I love you's and affection, I failed to realize that being adored was not the same as actually being in love. I felt guilty for misleading Bryce down a path I clearly was not invested in; I had used him to make myself feel better and in turn, had broken his heart. I realized that a boyfriend was not the solution to my problems. What I really needed to do was address not feeling worthy enough to find a boyfriend. I had felt the need to prove to myself that I was desirable and Bryce was the innocent bystander destroyed in my mission.

It was that moment when I learned my first of many very

important lessons in settling. There will be a time when I crave attention, and I will always find at least one person to give it to me. Though this guy may pursue me and make it easy to get involved, before taking any next steps in going further I would now take a step back and assess the situation. If I'm not thinking about this guy day in and day out, if he grates on my nerves, if I find myself thinking about other people when I'm with him, then I'll bow out of the relationship early, or better yet, pass on it entirely. It can be painful at first, and potentially hard to explain, but in the long run, it always turns out better. It would take a while for the effects of this of a breakup to wear off, but eventually Bryce moved on and my life returned to normal.

A few years later, when I met Jason, I had no intention of making him my boyfriend. We became friends over months of spending time together and I eventually found myself attracted him in a "more than friends" type way. I eventually accepted an invitation back to his house and once we officially crossed the line from friends to more-than-friends, our relationship took its seemingly natural course into couple-dom. This set the stage for our relationship; because we already knew each other so well, we never went on dates. Instead, he would call me up and say, "Hey, want to come over? I'll pick you up and make you dinner, then we can just relax in my room and watch the new movie I picked up." This was typically followed by hooking up and then falling asleep. Though I yearned for more romance and connection, the offer seemed better than being alone and single. Plus having a regular dose of sex kept me coming back despite the lack of everything else. Even though our proposed routine wasn't mind-blowing, the thought of having somebody to spend time with was alluring.

Our nights, however, never lived up to the already low standard set. Jason would pick me up and we would go to the store together to buy ingredients to make dinner. We would then go back to his place and he would immediately sit down with his roommate to watch the football/basketball/baseball game, while I retreated to his room to find *anything* else to watch. Hours later Jason would holler back to his room to see if I wanted dinner yet. Finally he would make his way to his bedroom and we would have routine sex before falling asleep.

Swoon.

Over and over promises of quality time and dinner making were dangled in front of me, and like an insane person, I kept expecting the night to go as originally offered. It never did, but I couldn't stop. I needed someone in my life so I stayed in this "relationship" even though I cried myself to sleep almost every night. I was constantly wondering why he didn't want to spend quality time with me. I tried a few times to force myself into the roommate bonding sports time, and felt all but invisible. He was too into whatever was on the TV to even notice that I was right next to him.

I continued on with Jason despite feeling empty and unfulfilled; I was lonely and I desperately wanted and needed someone to share my life with. I wanted to eat dinner with someone, wake up in the morning next to someone, have somebody to laugh with and vent to. Most of all, I wanted consistency. I started to wonder what was wrong with me and became riddled with self-doubt. I questioned whether I was too boring or annoying and why he seemed more interested in TV. I feared I wasn't attractive enough to make him want me more. I so was lost in trying to figure out what was wrong with me, that it took me far too long to realize that maybe I wasn't the problem.

On the surface I was getting what I asked for—to not be single —so it was hard to recognize that while I was "with" Jason, I was still very much alone. What I really yearned for was quality time—activities done together, chosen together and enjoyed together; I didn't want to be an afterthought in somebody's life, next to college football and MLB finals. When my in-couple loneliness was too much to bear, I finally broke it off. Jason was confused at first, but didn't really fight to keep me in his life. Freshly back to my single life, I bought myself an extensive movie collection and started making my own dinners. I was still lonely, but I realized that being lonely on my own terms was something I could handle and it was much better than being with someone who made me feel invisible.

After the sting of the breakup wore off, I started to like the time by myself. The fact that I had control over my alone time helped me feel more at ease.

It became obvious that I had been fooling myself thinking that because I wasn't technically single, I wasn't still painfully alone. Having just anybody in my life would never be the magic elixir to cure my loneliness. There was nothing worse than being unable to connect with the man that was lying right next to me every night. Instead of spending that time unhappy in a situation I couldn't control, I figured it was better spending the time alone and investing in myself. By owning my alone time, rather than feeling like a victim to it, I started to realize my true worth. I felt completely and unapologetically selfish and used this time to indulge in what truly made me happy—whether that was eating a frozen pizza while watching Netflix or working on my newest creative idea.

My next stint in low standard love came from left field with a guy I ran into periodically around the city. This guy embodied Spike Lee—sharp, irritating, opinionated, 5'4"—but, because of my incredible losing streak in love, I was determined to be open to everything, even Spike Lee.

After a few casual run-ins, he suggested we get together sometime. Though I wasn't completely sold on the idea, I remained open-minded and agreed. At the time, my life felt stagnant, and while Spike didn't exactly look like my ideal match, he was successful. I was striving to make something of my career and was happy to entertain somebody who was thriving.

To my surprise, we started out pretty adorably. Spike would swing by on his way home from work and we would sit outside and talk. He would call if he had a quick break and I would spontaneously meet him for lunch. Spike always had an air of urgency, which intrigued me. I looked forward to hanging out with somebody who had the drive to move forward in life and daydreamed about having a power couple type relationship.

However soon my idea of who Spike should be didn't match the man I was getting to know. Warning signs of him being selfish and dismissive started popping up, but I brushed them off and continued to focus on the positive—that he was successful, ambitious and was interested in me. The red flags piled up, but I continued to justify them. He would often stop listening to me in the middle of my stories to read his latest e-mail, but I fantasized about the day where we'd both reading important e-mails over the table. I would rearrange my schedule to be available when he had a free moment, even if it meant putting off something in my own life, because I was grateful he thought of me in the moments he had spare time. Sometimes we would go on walks at night, which always took longer than I really had time for, but because I wanted to glean as much as I could from him, I never spoke up. What I wanted to say was, two hours is enough, I have to get back to working on my own projects—instead I continued to invest in what I thought could be our future.

I poured all my energy into him. Though it wasn't going exactly as I had planned, I was willing to make a few sacrifices—like not getting a lot of attention—because I had found somebody who had the ambitious qualities I was attracted to. After a few weeks of me patiently playing the role I thought he wanted, he brought up the subject of a relationship. I was eager to have him all to myself, thinking that maybe if we were "official" he would commit more attention to me and I would be less of an afterthought. What came next was worse than being rejected. He offered to be my boyfriend, under one condition—that our relationship remain a secret. His reasoning was that his career might suffer if he was seen to have a girlfriend.

I was shocked and hurt. He once again made me feel like an afterthought and more, a dirty little secret. He never once considered how his offer of being a private girlfriend might have made me feel, and like all the warning signals predicted, it was completely based in selfish agenda. That final straw that was the slap in the face I needed. I finally realized I was only an addendum to his incredibly self-centered and busy life, and no matter how successful he was, he wasn't interested in connecting with me. Spike would never be the other half to my power couple. He wasn't invested in my well being, which became counterintuitive to why I chose an ambitious success seeker; I wanted to find a partner who could rise with me, not leave me in the dust.

After stepping back from the situation I saw that I had been making excuses for him all along—he used his ambition as an excuse to be a dick and those two things were not synonymous. My standards of how I wanted to be treated and what I truly wanted in a partner had become danger-ously low—enough for me to realize I needed to break free. I declined Spike's offer to be his secret girlfriend and took my wounded ego back to the single's scene, a place I was beginning to dread more and more. Each time I thought about being single, I thought of how hard it was to find a guy I actually liked, and more, one who would like me back. But I was able to grasp the little morale I had left and stand up for myself.

After this experience I recounted all the times I made up guys' personalities for them. Maya Angelou has famously said, "When somebody shows you who they are, believe them the first time." This advice finally sunk in after I got some distance from the Spike fiasco. From the beginning he had displayed the qualities of somebody who was self-centered and had no intention of being in a relationship; in my desperation to find the other half to my power couple, I had disregarded everything he was showing me and made him a completely different person in my head. I had wasted valuable time and energy on him and the thought of "us" that I could've used on myself. I imagine if I had taken those hours and used them to work on things to make myself successful, I would never need him to lift me up anyway. Through the effort of trying to make a relationship happen, I started to get smaller. I didn't defend myself, and I didn't check him when he was being disrespectful, and that made me less of a woman than I knew I was.

As I looked back on every time I had settled in a relationship. I hung with guys for far too long just because I was bored or lonely. I gave them the energy I should've been giving to my friends, my family and myself. I overlooked what I knew deep down inside, because I didn't want to be single.

It was at that moment I swallowed a hard pill – that I might never be the girl that has a boyfriend. I may be single for 10 more years, even twenty. I may find love much later in my life, or I may never find that "one" person. I sat with the possibility that I may instead have little flings here and there providing me with other adventures and lessons.

So really the challenge was upon myself. Was I brave enough to be single? Was I really okay spending another night in my bed by myself? Once I let go of the idea that I was less than if I didn't have a man, I started to feel complete. Once I realized that I would be whole with or without a partner, it was easier to stick to my standards and stop settling for less than I wanted. As a single woman I finally got to a place where I recognized that I am in charge of whether or not a relationship is destined for the dumpster. If I didn't like the way things are going then I would be ready and willing to say goodbye, and understand that being alone is far better than being with someone I would lecture my best friend for being with.

To discover this newfound power I had to learn to be comfortable saying, "I'd rather be alone than in this situation." I had to wrap my head around that concept: I'd rather be SINGLE than to settle for less than I want and deserve. I'd rather be single than be treated like second best. I'd rather be single than to not be called back. I'd rather be single than to be one of 10 girls he's dating, I'd rather be single than to wait for him to change his mind about marriage/children/growing up/getting serious. These were hard realizations, but they were essential for true happiness. In the end, self-worth and confidence are where the power—or more specifically, the empowerment—lies. Once I found this confidence, I realized that being single wasn't so bad and sticking to basic standards was all up to me.

——— LESSON ———

Standing up for yourself and your standards leads to a sense of self-worth, self-confidence and in the end, more satisfaction out of life—single or not.

······ **HOMEWORK** ······

1. THINK OF YOUR PAST RELATIONSHIPS and write down the little and big ways you compromised what you wanted. Explore whether you were compromising for the benefit of relationship or you were compromising yourself and your worth. (i.e. did you put your clothes away instead of on the floor—compromise. Or did you settle for somebody who wanted to see other people when you wanted a commitment—compromising yourself).

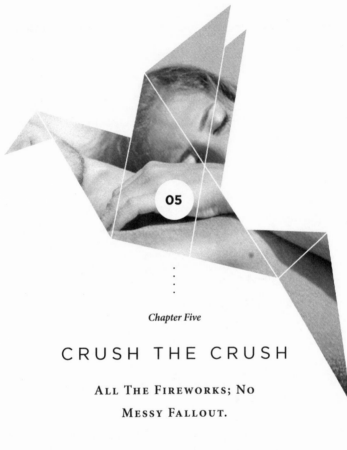

05

Chapter Five

CRUSH THE CRUSH

ALL THE FIREWORKS; NO MESSY FALLOUT.

E ven living a full, single life, occasionally, I get bored. While most of the time I don't miss the drama of emotion that can accompany liking somebody, I sometimes yearn for the pick-me-ups—the sweetness of thinking about somebody, the blushing, and the overall flirty behavior. Somewhere along the way I discovered how to teeter in between worlds, and identified the perfect approach to having a crush that brought me all the high notes of liking somebody but omitted the difficulties of a having real relationship.

I spent many of my early single years fixating about the future outcome of every crush; one crush in particular, was agonizing. Will, who ran in my same circle, was always playful and flirtatious. It seemed that he went out of his way to be near me and would continually find a way to make contact if we were sitting next to each other. He lavished me with flattery and twinkled his eyes at me when nobody was looking. I loved all the attention and was constantly electrified with excitement. Soon I was addicted and eager for what was next. The more our flirtations advanced, the more I thought about how perfect we would be together; it killed me that he wasn't making a definitive move to be my man.

I wanted to advance things with Will but was terrified to broach the subject. Instead, I started to analyze every small notion to determine if he really liked me and therefore might be my future boyfriend. My best observation skills went toward deconstructing his body language down to the most imperceptible movements. I constantly analyzed the distance between us, deciphering if he stood closer to me than to anybody else. I hung on to every "Babe or "Cutie" out of his mouth and studied it like it was gospel.

After two months of exhausting my friends with investigative reports of every small detail Will displayed throughout the day, one of my friends put it to me straight.

 "This is madness, you need to just talk to him."

She challenged me to call and ask him what was going on between us. The idea evoked a fear greater than any I had felt before. I thought of all the things that might go wrong: being rejected outright and him not liking me back, looking like a crazy girl who was way too attached, messing up our current situation and therefore losing the attention I was currently getting from him.

I swallowed my dread and vowed to her that I would call him Sunday morning. When the day arrived, I wanted to throw up. Of all the things I've done in my life, asking a guy if he liked me was the scariest. I rang him and when he answered, I spent the first 20 seconds speaking nonsense and generally being awkward. After a number of failed attempts to ease into the conversation, I went straight for it and blurted out "What are we? I'm trying to figure out if you like me and if you want more…"

He didn't.

Over the next few weeks our interactions changed and all of our flirtations came to a screeching halt. Every single one of my fears was realized; I definitely scared him off, I definitely made our friendship uncomfortable, I definitely said all the wrong things and rocked the boat. I definitely looked like a girl who was attached too soon. I definitely lost the attention that I used to get from him every day. The void left by the disappearance of our daily flirting was large and cold. It was then when I realized that perhaps what I wanted from him, I'd already had and by trying to push it forward, I'd lost it. As I analyzed the situation I realized that the lesson here looked eerily like the age old spiritual teaching– stay present. In life, and it turns out in crushes, worrying about the future outcome can ruin the current moment.

The everyday butterflies and coquetry were what I enjoyed the most. I didn't necessarily want a relationship; I merely got greedy with what felt good. Crushes put pep in my step, but it was easy to get lost down a slippery slope. So I determined the best way to not lose my footing was to stay in the moment and not think about the future. Sometimes a crush is just a crush and best left at that; over analyzing every little step would never be an accurate indication of what was to come. After a few more practice crushes, I had mastered the art, learned to stay present and savored the sweetness.

When it finally sank in that every guy I came across didn't have to be a candidate for my next boyfriend, a new world opened up. Guys I had previously not considered because they were unavailable, not my type, had a few undesirable qualities or were not geographically feasible were now open game for crushing on.

Soon I found a new enthusiasm for each day. I started to notice that almost everybody around me was crush-worthy in some form or another. Attractive qualities materialized in all my interactions with previously overlooked men. There was Trenton, a self-absorbed model, who was great at flirting and had a gift for making me feel really sexy. Jake was the nerdy type who stimulated my mind with his brilliance. Kendrick, not somebody I would normally be attracted to physically, was inspiring, ambitious, and always cooked me dinner. Having mini, nonchalant crushes dispersed throughout the week added up. Meanwhile I was free to go about my business when each interaction ended.

One of my favorite new non-crush crushes was Sebastian. Initially upon meeting, he irked me. His pace was excruciatingly slow and I didn't have the patience to talk to him, often brushing him aside. But once I realized I didn't have to adore him in order to appreciate him, I started to notice his lovable qualities. Sebastian was caring and incredibly self-aware, always mindful of making those around him happy. He was considerate and once I opened up to him, found out he was a phenomenal listener. Sebastian started to call me during his commute and while at first, I was thrown off at his random check-ins, I started to look forward to our top-of-the-morning heart-to-hearts. To my surprise, not all of his carefully deliberate speech was bland. As I started to pay attention, I noticed his deadpan humor and it finally registered that he was actually hilarious. Sebastian continually provided all the things I was currently missing by being single – he was attentive, entertaining, and made me feel better on my bad days, but I was careful to leave it at that and to not ruin it with wanting more—he had also been very clear that he didn't want to settle down and wasn't looking for a girlfriend. So I siphoned the good and avoided the messy.

Seeking out crush worthy qualities in people enhanced my appreciation for those around me and improved my daily life, which got a lot more gratifying and included tons of ego boosts and pick-me-ups. I became a more appreciative person; all in all, I was essentially seeing the best in people by pointing out their greatest qualities.

Once I learned to stay present in my crushes, and had expanded the pool of crush-worthy options, I was able to start reaping benefits of no-attachment infatuation, one of which was practice. Even with all my previous dating experiences, I was still a complete train wreck when it came to intimacy and interaction. I would often become flustered as soon as an attractive man came into near proximity. If I had feelings for somebody, my first instinct was to run away. And forget about thinking of anything cute or clever to say, because my mind would turn to mush. But using my crushes as practice helped me improve some of these unfortunate side effects.

One of my crushes, Brandon, redefined "love at first sight." He was the new guy at work and easily the most beautiful man I had seen. His style was impeccable, yet effortless. He wore a T-shirt that grazed his perfectly sculpted stature. Upon our first meeting, I scanned his features while trying to listen intently to who he was and why he was there. The introduction finally culminated with a handshake and I felt the world tremble when we touched. His grip was strong, yet respectful. His hands were manly and slightly rugged, which was a surprising divergence to how pretty he was. My life was about to get better if I got to look at this guy every day.

Later that afternoon, and to my delight, Brandon was as-
signed the desk across from me. My heart skipped a beat
when I realized that every time I looked up from my work, the
opportunity to take in beautiful scenery was now a reality.
After a few bouts of sustained across-desk eye contact,
he got comfortable and started flirting. As weeks went by,
our daily flirting got more intense and I secretly flipped out
when, he replied with "Thanks, Babe" during one of our conversations; my heart started pounding and my face flushed
hot pink and that would be the beginning of our zealous, yet
completely professional work relationship.

Months went by and Brandon and I continued straddling
the line between HR violations and newfound work "buddy"
status. We remained professional on the surface, but flirted
enough that it always felt as if we were sharing a secret
every time we interacted. This secret was hidden under-
neath every sentence, within every shared glance, and sub-
merged in all accidental and casual grazes.

Innocent peeks soon turned into electric eye contact. The
space between us shrank until daily affection became
natural. He would put his hand on my back as we spoke.
This affection was intermixed with easy flirting. We leaned
on each other for support and advice. So far, this was the

best relationship I had ever experienced. The only thing missing was the making out and having sex, but I was willing to forgo those satisfactions because all day, every day I became more and more fulfilled.

Through the slow burn of indulging in this crush, I was able to practice all the things that typically terrified me in a real relationship. I practiced letting my guard down. I worked on maintaining open and honest communication. I routinely took risks, whether it was a small one like reaching out to touch his arm, or a big one like inviting him to post work happy hour.

I also practiced being emotional and vulnerable. Being single, I had a tendency to fill my life with every thing else—work, friends, chores and personal projects; it was really nice to reignite feelings I put off for so long, and furthermore to indulge in them. Since I wasn't used to having butter-flies everyday, it was a stretch not to freak out about them. But eventually I stopped blushing every time we made eye contact and I was able to come up with witty comebacks instead of just giggling in response to our banter. Finding a level of comfort with him made me realize that big crushes were nothing to be terrified of. My take-away from all this was that practice makes perfect. Being single for long periods of time generally deteriorates most of my romantic skills, but finding somebody to rehearse with was a ton of fun with minimal risk attached.

Through each of these enlightening moments, I had come up with the perfect formula and had mastered the art of the crush: stay present, seek out the best qualities in everybody and practice. Following these key steps didn't ever bring a boyfriend into my life — nor did they intend to – but mastering them made my life a lot more interesting. The art of the crush is enjoying the moment and squeezing everything out of it—every emotion, every feeling of love, all the cuteness, banter and unique connections in order to make life a little more interesting.

—— LESSON ——

Boyfriends aren't the only option for feeling butterflies.

······ **HOMEWORK** ······

1. TO FILL THE VOID, find a crush and practice staying present (no hoping for the relationship to take off).

2. IDENTIFY AND WRITE DOWN GREAT QUALITIES in everybody you come across in a day.

3. PRACTICE FLIRTING. Here are some basics. Smile at somebody across the room. Close the distance between you and the person you're flirting with. Find little ways to reach out and make physical contact. Be the first to say something.

06

⋮

Chapter Six

KEEPING THE ROMANCE ALIVE

AN EXPERIMENT IN DATING MYSELF.

'll admit it. Sometimes being single sucks. Sitting alone in my bedroom, pretend shopping on Victoriassecret.com, and picking out what I would wear for my non-existent boyfriend was getting depressing. Buying lingerie felt point-less since I didn't have a man to wear it for. On the upside, I saved money; but the downside was that I never celebrated my hard-earned body in some really beautiful pieces.

As I sat in my basketball-center-sized sweats, a cutoff tee and a zip hoodie, my hair in a pony, I got fed up with how frumpy I was. My room was a mess; I had two almost empty coffee cups and three wine glasses on my night stand alone. I felt like one of those sad RomCom girls who lie in bed, demoralized after she gets her heart broken. The only thing I was missing was the quintessential pint of ice cream and of course, the broken heart. I gazed in admiration at the Victoria's Secret model's flowing hair and golden skin as she sensually sauntered down a majestic beach. Then I looked up into my closet mirrors and took in my reflection and decidedly non-majestic environment.

Nope. This had to stop.

"Listen Self, you can't go down like this. Single or not, this is no way for a successful, hot, motivated young woman to represent. You have to do better." And with that, I bought three items on VS and loaded the dishwasher.

I decided that if I had no man to speak of, and no one in the queue, I would take romance into my own hands. No sense in missing out on some beautiful celebrations in life just because I was flying solo.

In 3-5 shipping days, my VS lingerie arrived, but I didn't quite know what to do with it. "Should I just put it on? Then what?" I questioned whether I felt comfortable enough to just hang out in a sexy nighty. I also didn't want to go through a ton of effort to look smoking hot only to have nobody to acknowledge my efforts. I sat looking at my new gifts to myself and decided to just wing it. Not knowing quite what to do, I started by putting the cute panty, bra and garter set on. As I slipped it on I noticed the intricate lace detailing and delicate ribbons placed carefully on each of the pieces. It fit surprisingly well for a first attempt. However, as I stood there looking in the mirror I noticed the disconnect between the stunning outfit and my bare feet and stubbly legs. I had yesterday's make up on and my hair was pulled off my face. It was only about 8pm and I had a few hours before I was going to go to bed, so I decided to try and upgrade myself to Victoria's Secret Angel status.

As I hopped in the bathtub, I took it a step further and threw on some relaxing ballads and lit candles. Immediately, I felt more sensual. I slid into the tub and instead of rushing to get through my grooming routine, I lay there soaking in the surrounding warmth of the steamy water. The background music and quiet ambiance started to fill me with a sense of peace. It was so nice to take a moment to just be. I started to make a list in my head of all the things I had enjoyed that day. It was a short list because I had forgotten to stop and enjoy anything. I had been so busy going places and doing things, I barely remembered what my day had been about. I did remember two things though: The first moment I was grateful for was when my mother called me in the morning on my way to work. The second grateful moment was when a coworker told me I was the nicest person in the company. The warm water was flowing, as were the warm fuzzies. I reflected a bit more on forgotten moments during the previous week and started to realize that I had it pretty good in life.

A sexy Prince song came on the mix and I remembered why I was in that sensual bathtub in the first place. I shaved my legs and finished up with a shower. I got out and began to get ready like I had a date. I dried and curled my hair. I put on makeup, mascara and applied a red lip for good measure. After all was said and done in the bathroom I went back to my room and once again tried on my lingerie. Now, the only thing missing was a hot pair of heels. After I found the perfect pair and slipped them on, I took a long look in the mirror. What a difference! Not only was I polished, I was holding myself differently—confidently. I switched my hip to the side and struck a pose. Truth be told, it felt pretty awkward at first. My brain kept trying to tell me I was being silly. But I had done plenty of awkward things in my life and I knew I had better poses in me. So I threw out a couple more booty pops and hip switches until I found the one. Yep the pose that made me feel like I could give the Victoria's Secret model a run for her money, as long as I was accompanied by awesome lighting.

After posing in the mirror for about 15 minutes, I was starting to feel better and much less silly than I had felt initially. I wasn't sure what else to do after my posing session so I went and turned on the TV. I sat luxuriously in my lingerie on my comfy sofa and watched Pretty Little Liars for the next hour. I noticed that during the show my legs felt really soft, I just ended up rubbing them and feeling how curvy my hips and thighs were.

What was normally a boring TV session had turned into really great quality time with myself. I reminded myself that I was beautiful and I appreciated all my hard work and natural gifts. I had dressed up for myself, and because of this, felt a boost in my self-worth. If there was anybody worth dressing up for it was me.

This newfound spirit carried over into the next morning and showed up big time as I stepped—no, strutted—into work. My coworkers took notice and I received approximately three more compliments than usual, which further perpetuated my enthusiasm for myself.

After a long day at work I finally called it a wrap and started to pack my stuff up to head home. Since there were some coworkers lingering nearby, I invited them to go grab dinner. They unfortunately all had post work plans and I thought to myself, "Right, well now what? I definitely don't want to get dolled up to watch PLL again tonight."

With this thought I made a decision to be anywhere but home in the next two hours. I thought about the gym but didn't have my gym clothes with me. My next thought was motivated by the grumble in my stomach—dinner! While going out to dinner alone didn't necessarily scare me, or make me feel like a loser, it did sound pretty boring. But I was on a mission to romance myself and that meant treating myself to something nice. I decided to find a restaurant with a really great view so I could gaze out at my beautiful city instead of my dinner plate.

I opened up Yelp, searched for restaurants with a view, and

off I went. I chose a spot on the top floor of a hotel over-looking the skyline. I felt from this vantage point I would be able to get perspective on what was outside my little world of work and home, and feel like a total boss. After all, most successful people seemed to end up in places with views.

I arrived at the hostess station and she politely but also a little irritatingly didn't acknowledge that I was ready to be seated. I could've been making it up, but it seemed like she was waiting for my date. I stepped forward to her and grabbed her attention and asked to be seated. She replied, "You have to wait until your entire party is here before I can seat you."

I felt like a feminist volcano starting to boil, but quickly took a breath and calmly replied, "My party's here; it's just me" It felt empowering to say that out loud. This empowerment prompted me to add, "I'd like something with a view, please."

The hostess looked at me for a few seconds and then she smiled ever so slightly and led me through the dining room. My girl did well and the view from the seat she chose was spectacular! I sat down and put my phone face down on the table and took it all in. As I overlooked the city, I felt like I was king of the world, watching over everybody. I started to stare at the lights and wonder what was happening inside each of the buildings. Were people still working? Were they making dinner? Alone? With somebody? Were they fighting? Loving? Or floating by in life doing neither? I thought of how I had just been floating by in life lately—routine actions and routine interactions, day in, day out. Wasting my time.

I felt as if I hadn't been paying attention in life. As I tried to recall the past month, it was difficult to remember anything significant. It felt as if I had gone through the entire time looking down at the ground or in my phone. I felt ashamed and regretful that I had wasted so many days not noticing anything. I looked out the window and remained in my thoughts—looking but not seeing—and I realized, "I'm doing it again!" Even with this beautiful view outside, I was still completely in my head and not noticing what was around me—I was being a terrible date. I immediately snapped out of my daydreams and reset my focus to take in the room and noticed what was happening in my immediate surroundings.

There were business meetings, dates, and friends eating dinner and talking over drinks. Some people had the straight up stuff, brown liquor on the rocks in a classic tumbler, while others had more elaborate cocktails ranging in complexity from Pisco Sours to Mai Tais. I concentrated hard on each table for about five minutes trying to get a read of the energy between the patrons. I didn't make up any stories this time; I just observed. I started to notice subtle changes in body positioning, sideways glances, distracted cell phone checking. I perceived that each of these actions when strung together portrayed exactly where that person was at the time. Without hearing any words in the conversation I knew who was having the time of his life and who was ready for the bill. I could tell who had had one too many drinks and who was trying not to eat all of the dessert.

After observing the different people across the room, I caught eyes with an older gentleman at the next table over. He had been there with a woman, but was alone momentarily while she was assumedly at the bathroom. We connected glances and shared a small closed mouth smile and a nod. I held my gaze for about three seconds longer than what is typical for a shared glance between strangers and in those three seconds I was able to connect with this man. I didn't get any sweeping revelations during this time. I didn't all of a sudden know his life story, but I acknowledged him and in turn, he acknowledged me.

My meal came out and I turned my attention to my food. It was a little strange just eating and sitting there. For a girl who typically washed down cheese and crackers with wine for dinner, I wasn't quite sure how to savor my meal, but was open to the new experience of enjoying food for nothing more than the meal; no company, no work—just food. I went all the way through dessert just eating; quiet with my thoughts and myself. I continued to take in my surroundings and soon, time had passed and I found myself calm and relaxed. It was a welcome change of pace from my frantic day.

I went home and reflected on yet another phenomenal ending to a regular day. After day two of "romancing" myself, I realized that by waiting for a boyfriend to experience these things with, I was holding myself back from some of the best stuff in life. Even though I didn't really know what I was doing at first, and my intentions weren't exactly to pamper myself, investing this precious me-time was turning out to be the best thing I'd done in a while. This was an eye opening revelation. I decided to continue the week with enriching experiences all by myself.

The following morning while I got ready for work I put on Beyoncé and had the ultimate dance party. I danced like nobody was watching because, clearly, nobody was. I practiced all the moves I wanted to try out but was always too afraid to. I stretched my splits out. I flipped my hair. I strutted across my room like I was ready for a dance battle.

What I experienced was pure joy and unbridled freedom. All in about 15 minutes. I was a little late to work, but as I arrived, I was shining. My coworkers returned my enthusiasm. Later in day, during the mid-afternoon, post-lunch slump, I got brave. I decided that everybody needed to feel the same passion I had awakened earlier that morning. I turned on my favorite Michael Jackson song and single-handedly started another dance party. This time people were watching, yet I was able to bring my uninhibited dance moves to the party. I was a catalyst for others to feel great too. I was an inspiration for everybody to let go and to feel good. It felt like a whole other side of me was alive. I felt powerful and influential. I felt awesome.

Throughout this pivotal week, I had some monumental breakthroughs. I realized that I was enough to make my life complete. Up until this point, I had done a fantastic job building my career, my home and my social life—it was now apparent that building myself was equally important—and that was solely up to me. I didn't want to have to rely on anybody—not a boyfriend, not friends, not family—to be truly satisfied. This didn't mean I would ostracize everybody in my life to become a strong, independent woman, but it meant that I took responsibility for how my life felt. Was it a happy place to be? Fulfilling, fun, intriguing? If I couldn't find friends to go out to dinner, I didn't want that to stop me from enjoying that particular luxury of life. If I didn't have anybody to go dancing with, I wanted to know that I could still express the pure joy of dancing anywhere—whether it was in front of my closet mirrors or at a self-started dance party at work.

When I started investing in myself, it showed. It was apparent when I walked down the street; it showed up when I was with my friends. And furthermore, it was contagious. To thrive as a single woman, it became imperative that I needed to take care of myself and find ways to make my life amusing. I solidified that I was in control of how satisfying my life would be, so I vowed to do at least two experiments a week to keep my tank full and to maintain this high I had discovered. Though the actions I took, whether I was spoiling myself, dancing or dining alone, may have seemed frivolous, they were essential. If I had the confidence to be myself when it was just me, then I was on the road to being that same awesome woman with the rest of the world.

——— LESSON ———

Don't wait for somebody else to indulge in the finer things in life. Become the person you want to spend 100% of your time with.

······ **HOMEWORK** ······

1. DRESS UP IN YOUR FANCIEST LINGERIE and pose in the mirror until you find the one position that makes you feel like a goddess.

2. TREAT YOURSELF TO DINNER in an inspiring location. Take note of all your surroundings both in the distance and one foot away. Take a moment to not think and just observe without expectations.

3. DANCE PARTY FOR ONE. Dance like nobody's watching. Take a shot or two if you have to get warmed up.

4. BONUS, START A DANCE PARTY at work or other lame environment that needs an energy boost.

07

Chapter Seven

LET'S TALK ABOUT SEX, BABY

SEX AND EMPOWERMENT AS A SINGLE WOMAN.

Sex can be a tricky subject when single. While it's great to have the freedom to hook up with anybody I want, I've confronted plenty of issues in the realm of single sex. I've fought through the stigma of feeling like a slut for having multiple partners. I've gotten my feelings hurt when I mistook sex for intimacy. I've faced incredibly long droughts and have felt hopeless when presented with a plethora of less than ideal options. But I've navigated through singledom and ended up making a set of rules that are perfectly fit for me.

One of the first lessons I picked up early in my single life was that sex and a relationship aren't synonymous and one doesn't necessarily determine the other. This was a crucial distinction to make and took a few missteps and a harsh reality check to figure it out. The ultimate teacher of this was Mike. I had developed a huge crush on him; he was everything—handsome, athletic, funny and smart. On top of that, Mike and I had been flirting and exchanging clandestine double entendres and innuendos for a year. I constantly daydreamed about our future relationship. One day our flirting finally caught fire and he initiated an informal date when he text me the ultimate code phrase, "Want to watch a movie?"

I went over to his apartment and we did the inevitable make out turned sexual encounter. Though he had a beautiful body and we had had a year's worth of sexual tension to work out, the sex felt surprisingly distant and lackluster. I was stunned at how distant it felt; it was not at all like I imagined it would be, but even so, I chalked it up to first time jitters. After it was over, he gave a clear hint that it was time for me to leave. I used the bathroom on the way out and was caught off guard at the sight of eight toothbrushes in a cup by the sink. The outright audacity of a guy to display the possibility of up to eight regular overnight guests was a glaring omen, but because I had hoped so much for our future, I chose to laugh it off and assume that he just had an obsession with brushing his teeth. My delusions won over and I went home feeling victorious about starting something new with this incredibly hot man.

Over the next few days I proactively tried to nail down follow up plans with him, even if those plans just included another "movie night," but was continually brushed off. After about five repeated attempts and subsequent rejections, my ego was thoroughly wounded and I gave up all hope of our future together.

This was the first time I mistook sex for intimacy. I was really confused and hurt after I realized Mike didn't want much more to do with me than to close the loop. He wanted a finale to our flirting—to cross me off the list. I had thought after a year of build up, the sex would've meant more, as it did to me, but the reality was that I was just a one night stand; that reality cut deep. This wouldn't be the last time I slept with somebody hoping it would turn into something more. But I eventually realized that a relationship isn't determined by having sex and if I was having sex only in the hopes of starting a relationship, I would be disappointed every time.

I started to ask myself what I was really after. Once I learned to identify my own desires, whether it was for just sex or for more, like a relationship or companionship, it was easier to make judgment calls when encountered with situations like the one with Mike. If I only wanted a hook up, there was no harm in going for it, but if I was looking for a more emotional and lasting connection, it was probably best to hold off and heed the signs.

Getting comfortable with the idea of sex for sex's sake was a process. I didn't wake up one morning suddenly liberated from the confines of social judgment and personal guilt. As women, we are often taught to think of sex differently. Every part of it, from our first time to how many partners we have, is a weighty subject. At first, it was hard to see sex as a standalone subject, but after first identifying my own feelings, it was easier to figure out how to handle those feelings. If I felt like I was lonely and wanted companionship and emotional intimacy, then sex probably wasn't going to solve the problem. But if I was bored and wanted to feel excitement and physical intimacy, then sex was a fine solution. Because of this distinction, I was able to enjoy sex for what it was. It was no longer weighed down with mental baggage regarding the subject.

But even though I was now able to enjoy sex for sex, it didn't mean I was having it regularly. I would go through long phases when there was no action in sight. Whenever it had gone too long to bear, I would call on my good friend Nick. One night, after a long dry spell, I reached out with a text that just slightly varied from the "let's watch a movie" offer. He was obliging and invited me over. I arrived at his place and was pleasantly informed that his roommate was out on a date. It had been a while since our last hook up, so at first I was a little shy. While we sat side by side on the couch actually just watching the movie, I had a fierce internal debate on whether or not I should make a move. On one hand I definitely wanted to hook up and it's not like it would've been our first time. On the other hand, he wasn't making any moves either so I was unsure if he still wanted to hook up with me. While I was preoccupied mentally weighing out each side, his roommate came home with his new date and promptly took her upstairs.

Nick and I looked at each other with raised eyebrows and burst out with a quiet laughter that broke the ever present, albeit invisible and awkward barrier between two people who sit on the couch to watch movies. And with one swift shift in positioning, we promptly started making out. Then after a little of that, I broke the we're-going-to-have-sex-and-not-just-make-out barrier and reached further below the belt line. He paused, looked at me and said, "Are we really going to have sex?" My answer? "Uuuuuhhhh yes, but only if that's okay with you."

"Here?" he questioned.

"Can you be quiet?" I countered.

Nick responded with an unsure half nod, half shake. I took that as a solid no, he couldn't be quiet and responded, "How about the sauna?"

Not all of my friends or friends-with-benefits have saunas in their apartments, but he did and so we quickly evaluated the pros and cons.

Pros: private, quieter, unconventional and creative.

Cons: possibly awkward and uncomfortable, less than ideal temperature—even when not turned on fully.

The pros outweighed the cons and into the sauna we went. The temperature was definitely was warmer than the average room, but bearable enough to ignore. We immediately started making out again and getting undressed without missing a beat.

I left his place feeling refreshed, confident and satisfied. It was invigorating to have no other expectations than feeling good, whatever that looked like. My arrangement with Nick taught me that sex could be fun and spontaneous if that's what I was after. While I was single, I took full advantage of the freedom to hook up with anybody I wanted for whatever reason made me feel good. The important standards to adhere to were that I wasn't hurting anybody else and, most importantly I wasn't hurting myself. I discovered is that it was okay to just desire sex. Even when I felt comfortable with and attracted to somebody I was sleeping with, by not placing expectations on sex other than satisfaction in the moment, I ended up having a lot more fun with it.

Even in the midst of my sexual liberation, I also learned that just because everybody else seemed to be having crazy single sex, didn't mean that I had to. There seemed to be an ever present expectation that single people were out having tons of wild escapades. Mostly, I think this was a grass-is-greener fantasy made up by my married friends who might've been bored in their monogamous lives. But as a single woman I found it important to not fall victim to this expectation, and figure out what was comfortable for me.

One night I needed a ride home from a bar, so I called my go-to man du jour, Jack, and he came to get me. Jack had an incredible backyard area and promptly started a fire in the outdoor pit. I was dressed up and feeling pretty cute. That plus the fact that I was little cold made for a great reason to immediately cuddle up with him. I casually hinted about how chilly I was to get him to rub my arms and my bare legs, which led to a lot more touching, some kissing on my neck, a bit of making out, and then well, the rest. This nighttime escapade ended up fulfilling a long-standing fantasy of mine, which was having a racy night outdoors by a fire.

Jack had fantasies of his own, and after we had moved inside, he broached the subject of some bondage. There was some piping around the ceiling of his basement bedroom and he suggested we put those, and some rope to good use. I considered the proposal; in theory I thought the "idea" of being tied up sounded fun, but when it came right down to it—the moment of truth—I couldn't go through with it. There was something about the situation that made me unsettled—perhaps it was just a little too adventurous for me at that time. I wanted to have sex with him, a lot of it, and I wanted to have fun, but I also knew I wanted to be comfortable with and in control of my sexual experiences.

This was important for me to learn and to take with me into any sexual encounter: just because I had called someone with the primary intention of hooking up didn't mean I had to do whatever that person wanted. Part of becoming confident with sex and my choices as a single woman was recognizing that how far I go is entirely my choice.

I hit a point in my singledom where after so many casual hookups it started to feel obligatory to have sex, like checking a box—yep, we hooked up because we are "grown ups" and that's what "grown ups" do. It seemed like sex was the only thing on the menu. I felt like initiating a kiss was usually mistaken for an open invitation to go all the way. And if I didn't want more, I would have to thoroughly explain all the reasons I didn't want to have sex just then. I would be met point counterpoint to each time I threw out a reason I didn't want to hook up. Eventually the atmosphere would become so deflated that the only comfortable next step would be to leave. But as I grew more and more comfortable in my single woman skin, I started to stand for what I was truly looking for in that moment, which sometimes was just some innocent kissing.

When I first started hanging out with a new guy, James, there was really no possibility of a relationship, so we kept it pretty low key. I went over to his house, we got cozy and he made his move. As we made out, he, characteristically and unapologetically tried to go further. I stopped him, but kept it playful and we continued kissing. After a few more of his failed attempts at this playful cat and mouse game, I decided to definitively clarify, "I'm not going to have sex with you yet."

He inquired, "Why not? You know we're going to eventually."

I countered, "Perhaps, but this is way more fun."

I geared up for another battle and prepared to thoroughly kill the mood if it meant standing my guard. However he pondered for a moment, and surprisingly replied, "Yeah, you're right. This is more fun." I wasn't prepared for the curve ball he threw; I thought he would get bored or frustrated, but instead he accepted it and we dove back onto first base.

Our canoodling got more intense and I finally felt the butterflies I had been missing so much. Without the pressure of going any further than kissing, we got much more creative and started to discover each other. Our kisses went from playful to lingering to deep and hit all the notes in between; each of these kisses I had been previously glazing over in the race to the end.

Without the obligatory hook up, I was brought back to high school innocence and we both got a healthy dose of sexual frustration. Additionally, making out allowed me to test drive my new love interest before making any hasty decisions. I was pleasantly surprised by not only his tenderness, but also by his ability to be patient. I found out that to him, enjoying the moment was more important than "scoring." As I left that evening, I realized that besides the physical awakening I rediscovered by not having sex, my mind and my imagination were now piqued as well. Leaving unfinished business on the table made me way more excited than any physical activity had done in a while. The butterflies persisted; I was left wanting more. Rather than checking a box and moving on, just like with my regular to-do list, leaving one thing unchecked stayed on my mind the rest of the day. As a woman I pretty much have never had a hard time finding sex, which became problematic when I wanted to be challenged because I loved the chase. Even though I had to fabricate it myself, I was able to recreate anticipation and excitement.

During my sexual evolution I've realized that if I don't want to do something crazy, sleep with a ton of men or even have sex at all, it's okay; I finally felt empowered to make that decision. The opportunity in being single is really doing whatever I want when it comes to sex. If that's flying from the ceiling or being locked in closets or just making out fully clothed—it's my prerogative. I wasn't going to let pressure from society, friends or a guy sway me from getting what I really wanted.

—— **LESSON** ——

Sex is your prerogative. Do what you feel comfortable with and don't forget to have fun.

······ **HOMEWORK** ······

1. THE NEXT TIME YOU'RE THINKING ABOUT having sex with a new person, determine what your end game is. If it's a relationship, realize that sex may not get you there. But if it's just for satisfaction, be safe and go for it.

2. MAKE A LIST of what you are and are not willing to experiment with. Find your boundaries and don't be afraid to stand up for them.

3. NEXT TIME YOU'RE HOOKING UP, practice asking for what you really want. Say it out loud and confidently.

08

Chapter Eight

CHANGING YOUR MIND

HOW TO BE CONFIDENT IN YOUR DECISION-MAKING. OR NOT.

On the path to becoming my most outstanding, single, happy and independent self, I needed to learn to be okay with changing my mind. On the surface it seemed like an easy task; I change my mind daily on so many things. I change my outfit at least four times before I actually leave the house. One day I'll have a crush on my best guy friend, and the next I can't stand him. These instances of changing my mind are so fleeting that it seems odd that I would've ever felt hesitant to change my mind. But when it comes to bigger issues—and more specifically any time I've made a big deal about any such decision—my pride and fear of judgment keep me from veering right once I've already gone left.

One of the first times I noticed this phenomenon was during an embarrassingly painful phase in my dating life. I had an extraordinarily unlucky streak and after getting dumped repeatedly, I was completely over the whole dating experience. The coup de gras was when twice in a row, even though after a couple promising weeks of dating, I was dumped unceremoniously. The ending to both of these relationships was eerily alike and went something like, "Things are getting a little too serious. You're really special; I feel like we have a really great connection; I've enjoyed getting to know you; this isn't personal…"

While it was a nice way to say it's not you it's me, I became incredibly fed up with the dating scene. I was frustrated and confused about why I kept getting dumped. And even more, I was tired of throwing myself forward, getting attached and then being left crushed and crying at the end. I could not imagine putting myself through that one more time, maybe ever. Eventually the tears and frustration turned into anger and in a night out with my girlfriends, I made a bold and sweeping statement—I would be taking a permanent break from dating and dramatically prepared myself for months in a sexual wasteland.

Forty-eight hours later I realized that there was NO way I was letting a couple guys who were clearly idiots get the best of me and I secretly logged back on to OK! Cupid. Even though two days earlier I had no desire to go through all the motions of meeting someone new, possibly liking them, and opening myself up to be hurt again, I began to second guess my bold strike from dating. I questioned my decision to give it up, realizing it was mostly driven out of anger and that it probably wasn't the best solution to my dating woes. I was hesitant to tell my friends I'd put myself back on the market because I was afraid they'd think I was foolish for flip-flopping and for going right back to the place that had destroyed me just a few days earlier.

When I finally did tell my friends that I was back on the hunt, with no hesitation, they responded with support and encouragement—just as they had when I told them I was done with dating forever. I didn't know what I was so worried about. I had never worried about admitting to someone that I changed my mind about liking spinach, or if I suddenly got sick of my new favorite song. But for some reason, when it came to emotional decisions, I found it more difficult to accept that it was okay to change my mind. Even so, my friends were a perfect demonstration that this dramatization was in my head. My friends were there to listen and even if I'd made a big deal about my dating distasters, they were awesome friends and accepted me through all my nonsense and emotional breakdowns. I realized that I should never have felt foolish for making a huge scene about giving up dating then recanting my declaration. In the end everybody wanted me to be happy, and if that meant supporting me through a million more rejections, then they would do just that. They didn't judge me or make me feel bad for changing my mind.

This lesson really started to sink in when I watched my friend Emma struggle with her most recent long-term relationship. She had a few previous unsuccessful attempts at love before she finally found a relationship that worked for a while. She and her boyfriend were happy and carefree for two years before it started to unravel. A break up seemed inevitable, but Emma, already having two failed relationships hanging over her head, was afraid of failing yet again. At first, she was even embarrassed to talk about it with friends and family—afraid that admitting trouble in paradise would be admitting her own shortcomings. Emma didn't want to be judged and worried that another break up would mean that something was wrong with her; she feared that it would signify that she couldn't "succeed" at a relationship. This fear kept her in this less than ideal situation for an extra year where she was constantly unhappy.

As a bystander to this situation I realized how easy it was to let our egos play tricks on us. Our egos fool us into thinking that it would be far better to be unhappy than to fail at something. Our egos persuade us to pretend everything is all right so that we won't be judged for struggling. From an outside perspective, it was excruciating seeing her go through the process when the solution was as simple as deciding to leave the relationship—of course that would come with it's own challenges, but taking the first step would be the catalyst to positive change. It was eye-opening to watch Emma wrestle with the feelings of failure and seeing how trivial it was to worry about what other people think when her own happiness was on the line. And as her friend I would always support her no matter how many breakups she went through.

Emma finally cut the cord on their relationship and I witnessed her immediately blossom from under the dark clouds she had been living under. Her fears of failure or judgment were no longer a consideration. Emma realized that her anxiety was unwarranted and finally felt the happiest and freest she had felt in a year. The change was almost instantaneous.

This had a lasting effect on me. It was one thing to go through this discovery for myself and try to let go of my pride, but witnessing somebody I was close to fight this battle solidified how unproductive being afraid to change one's mind is. I was able to witness the tricks her mind played on her. I was able to see how easy it was to let go and move on once she decided to make a change. I realized that happiness, above all, was most important and just as I was encouraging Emma to pursue her happiest life, I should always remember to do the same, despite how it feels in the moment. This lesson stuck with me.

Though fear of judgment was a main motivator when deciding to change my mind. It wasn't the only factor that ever weighed in during these types of situations, and love wasn't the only area in which I questioned my decisions. If I'd invested a lot of time or money in something that wasn't working out, it was hard to know when to throw in the towel. During times like these, motivational phrases echoed in the back of my mind about how quitters never win and winners never quit. While this may have been true, I also discovered that perhaps winning didn't always equate happiness.

As an eager young adult, I was always excited to take a bite out of life and decided to start my own business. I had no interest in hearing any sort of cautionary tales or warnings of being prudent, and I charged forward with fervor. Not only had I declared I would open a business, I decided to do so in four months. In that time I secured a loan from family, leased a location and purchased everything I needed to open my business. While I acknowledge myself for being ambitious and taking a risk, I'll admit now that I was perhaps a little hasty.

Things started out okay, but once the excitement of actually creating the business wore off, I realized that running it wasn't really the glamorous life I imagined it would be. Not to mention I was now broke and had the added challenge of scrounging enough money to stay afloat and repay my loans. On top of these fundamental issues, my business partner was acting shady, which made me question my judgment. It started to become glaringly obvious that I had made the wrong turn and was pretty far down the wrong path. My everyday struggle started to wear on me and I became incredibly unhappy, lost and ashamed that I was failing. I questioned daily if working so hard for something that clearly felt wrong was the right thing to do even though I had always been taught that if I started something, I should finish it. I didn't want to be a quitter but I also didn't want to be unhappy or to live with a bad situation only because I felt I had to. I weighed my options to stick with the business and make it work, or to admit that in my hastiness, I had made the wrong move and get out.

This decision wasn't an easy one to make. There were obligations I had to address, which made a separation from my business feel much more like a divorce. I was worried about those who invested in me, who, even though I would pay back, I was afraid of letting down. I felt terrible that I was giving up on a dream that I convinced them to invest in. I was worried that the friends who had emotionally supported me throughout my struggle would feel their efforts were wasted if I decided to give up. I was about to be a big quitter and I had a lot of guilt when facing that thought. It was taking much more bravery to quit this venture than to start it.

Eventually I found the strength and made the decision to

leave. Contrary to other times I had changed my mind and was able to make an immediate shift in my life, this change was slow and bitter, but I finally felt I was on the right track. I realized that as hard as it was to switch directions, and no matter how stupid I felt, the outcome of my life was my responsibility; change wouldn't come unless I took the actions to make it so, even if that meant swallowing my pride.

This experience would stick with me. I knew that I could be faced with the same type of challenge any time in the future. This could be a business, such in that case, or it could be a relationship or marriage, a toxic friendship or an unhealthy environment. I knew there would be times when I've gotten in so deep that I'll feel there's no easy way out. The bottom line in any situation should always be to strive for happiness—even if that means trying a million different things and changing my mind a million and one different times to finally find it. While having the courage to change my mind didn't only affect my life when I was single, it allowed me to separate myself from a situation and remind myself what will truly make me happy. After all, single or taken, the most important thing I can do is enjoy life. Finding the freedom to change my mind allowed me to shift and adjust when needed to keep me on the path to achieving the most fulfilling life I can find. Life changes constantly; I've learned that it's not only okay, but also best if I change with it.

—— **LESSON** ——

*It's okay to change your mind, even if you've made a
big deal in your declarations.*

······ HOMEWORK ······

1. THINK OF A TIME you didn't want to change your mind because of your pride. Write about what it meant to change your mind. Who would you have disappointed? What fears were you facing?

2. WRITE DOWN WHAT LESSONS YOU LEARNED about yourself and those around you during these times. Was the outcome rewarding?

3. FOR EACH OF THESE EXPERIENCES respond to the following: if you had to go back and do it again, would you have done it differently?

Chapter Nine

TAKE A CHANCE, OR TWO

"Do One Thing Every Day That Scares you." -Eleanor Roosevelt

he journey to identify and then find what I really want out of life has taken a lot of trial and error. But with each trial and subsequent lesson, I continued to evolve into the best version of myself. The shy, cautious girl turned into the outgoing, friend-making, spontaneous woman. The complacent dreamer stopped yearning and took action to make her fantasies real. The lonely single woman eventually used alone time to pick up new habits and hobbies. The girl, who was constantly looking for validation from men, finally realized that the greatest sense of peace comes from fully loving herself. But each of these milestones would never have come to fruition without the first step. And big or small, that first step always involved an element of risk. It eventually became obvious that outside of my comfort zone was where all the magic happened and, being single, I had plenty of space and opportunity to make magic.

It took a while to connect the dots on this concept. For years, I didn't have the awareness to know that every small chance I took would change my future; I didn't consciously seek out risks in the name of transformation. I didn't actively pinpoint where I felt fearful and then decide to tackle it head on—that would all come later. Early on, what I had was a refrigerator magnet. It featured the infamous quote by Eleanor Roosevelt: "Do one thing every day that scares you." I saw it in a bookstore and I bought it for my sister because I thought being afraid was holding her back from being really happy. I wanted her to get crazy and stop worrying so much. But she never received the message (or magnet) of encouragement because I kept forgetting to mail it. It sat on my counter for months before I completely abandoned my lackluster efforts to send it and planted it squarely on my fridge. I didn't connect with the quote right away because I didn't think it was meant for me. I already felt like I had no fear—and I had proven it time and time again. I strayed away from my family religion when I was young, moved across the country many times; I was very capable of venturing into the unknown. Because I had taken so many big leaps in my life, I never really considered the possibility that I was still being held back by fear. I didn't realize that risk wasn't always glaring. I didn't recognize my fear because when it crept up, I had a justification for it. If I put off contacting a lead for a new job, I would convince myself that the effort would be futile. If I hesitated to talk to an attractive guy, I would justify my inaction persuading myself that he should pursue me instead. It took a while to see that my hesitation wasn't really procrastination or diversion; nine times out of ten it was fear. Even if I weren't admitting it, if the risk might have resulted in looking stupid or being rejected, I wasn't bold enough to take it, which was ironic because I was typically forthright. My friends and family always get an earful of exactly where I stood about everything. The difference was what was at stake when it was time to speak up. I had no problem talking in front of a group when I was prepared, like when I was teaching a dance class, or was presenting a project in school. Preparation made me feel confident and in control.

When speaking out on a whim, whether in front of a group of people, or sometimes just one really attractive one—I was a mess. In college I would envy people who would fearlessly share their thoughts in class. I wanted to participate, and I always had a ton of questions, but before speaking up, I would fight a battle in my head. I imagined the scenario would result in any number of failures: I would say something dumb, that all my words wouldn't come out right, that I would disrupt the flow of class and be a burden, or worse, be that annoying girl who's always asking all the questions. Each one of these possibilities flashed through my head while I tried to work up the nerve to say anything. Physically I would turn red and my heart pounded in anticipation. I would get so close to forming a word then chicken out, literally shaking in my boots. If somebody else were bolder and quicker to the draw than I was, I'd quickly back down and gratefully wait for the next opportunity. Eventually I would find the perfect crossroads of courage and timing and the words would finally make their way to life. My voice was shaky, and in some occasions my body would shiver like a Chihuahua. I felt like a freak. Did everybody go through this? Because this was a ridiculous process to go through just to ask a question in class.

Each time I survived this turmoil and over time I learned to suppress, or at least ignore my fight or flight responses in class. Even if I said something stupid, or my words came out jumbled, I began to realize that it doesn't really matter in the grand scheme of things. And a large majority of the time, I would actually ask smart questions and say something thought provoking.

Over time, beyond igniting my own courage, I noticed that sometimes, being the first person to speak could change the energy in a room. It was like breaking an invisible barrier, which opened the door for others to express themselves. After I had sparked a discussion, or gotten a few elephant in the room questions answered, others would tell me that by being vocal, I had inspired them to speak up as well. It was contagious.

I eventually learned that speaking up or asking questions was never about being right or looking smart; it was about contributing and moving the conversation forward, which is a lesson that applied almost everywhere.

Even though I was starting to feel all empowered and stuff,

this didn't mean I still wasn't scared to take this first small, albeit gigantic step. A friend and I were out enjoying some drinks when across the room I spotted the guy. He was brooding and wore a beanie and leather jacket in the most stylized bad boy way possible. His bone structure was impeccable and he had the kind of nondescript ethnicity that makes every woman daydream about spending countless hours tangled in the sheets on a deserted island. He. Was. Hot. I nudged my friend and discreetly pointed at him. "That guy," I said, unable to make any further sense of what I was thinking. She understood completely and urged me to go chat him up. But the gentle encouragement wasn't enough to get me to budge. I struggled to muster the courage to get off my chair, walk over to him and say hi. I felt like somebody might as well have asked me to give the presidential inauguration speech rather than go say hello; hello was terrifying. My mind was so mottled I couldn't even comprehend why or explain with any logical sense what I was so afraid of. It's not like I was often rejected from guys; in fact, I was almost never rejected. But even so I was paralyzed and just sat on my chair gazing from afar.

He got up to leave and the window of opportunity to spark a conversation was quickly closing. Even though I was rendered useless, I didn't want to lose this one. As he neared our table, which was on the way out, I put out an S.O.S. to my friend and quietly whispered, "HELP!"

Since her pride wasn't on the line, she effortlessly grabbed him and pulled him over to our table. The initial intro was just enough to kick me out of my paralysis and conversation and numbers were easily exchanged from there. Though the relationship didn't flourish with the hot guy from the bar, a few make out sessions did, and that was enough for me to feel rewarded. I was getting closer to taking the risks I wanted, even if it meant using a little help from a friend. With each time I overcame the crippling anxiety of making the first move, it was always much easier than I was making up in my head and I saw that the consequences weren't ever dire. All the humiliations I imagined never ever happened.

The next girls' night I was determined to be braver than the last. When I saw a guy I was interested in, I wanted to feel confident enough to talk to him. My friends and I ended up at a crazy karaoke spot, and the only guy I thought was cute in the whole place was the one serving me copious amounts of alcohol. Drink after drink I tried to work up the nerve to say something beyond, "Another gin and tonic, please." But with each pour, I still didn't have enough liquid courage to express my interest.

The bar was closing down; everyone was leaving. In fact, I had already walked out the door when I finally had had enough of being a wimp and turned myself around. I took a deep breath, walked back inside, and went straight up to the bar, looked cutie bartender in the face and said, "I think you need my number." I grabbed the nearest cocktail napkin, he handed me a pen, and voila! It was done and I felt victorious. About 30 minutes later when he was finished with his closing duties he gave me a call. Again, no Prince Charming at the end of this story, but a few weeks worth of flirting and a couple dates were more than enough for me feel proud of myself for making the first move. So far I was taking small steps out of my comfort zone and taking control of what I was experiencing in life.

I started to feel empowered and that's when I finally realized that risk really did beget reward. Instead of being trapped behind my fears—whether I was willing to admit it or not—I started to fathom how each connection I made could be the key to unlocking a new world. And by overcoming my fear to make a connection, I'd be inviting a lot of opportunities into my life. And that's ultimately what I was after: an abundant life of great connections, fun, friends and hopefully some adventure. I knew the secret to get more—all I had to do was step up and say something. And so, I figured that practice would make perfect and I started my self-initiated Elevator Challenge. I couldn't think of a more silent and awkward place than the elevator; if I could tackle this silence then I would be a real pro. I rode the elevator everyday at work, and being stuck in a sound vacuum for at least two minutes everyday with random people presented the perfect space and captive audience for my challenge. The first Monday morning after this declaration, I stepped in the elevator with my soon-to-be new friend. I pushed the buttons and felt the anxiety of breaking the silence. My elevator buddy immediately looked at his phone, even though there clearly was no cell service. The longer I waited the more the silence amplified. It soon felt awkward to even move. We reached my stop, fifth floor, the doors opened and the moment was gone. I had bombed at my first mission, but the feeling of regret for not seizing the opportunity was enough to fuel the fire for the next time.

Since I'm not one to give up after a failure, the next morning, I ramped myself up for my Elevator Challenge do over. As I walked into the elevator, subject number two arrived behind me. I pressed my button and asked, "What floor?" Elevator guy answered, "Six please." I kept the ball rolling and quickly followed up with, "Oh, where do you work?"

This was enough for me to keep the conversation going. I followed up with: What do you do? And, How long have you worked there? For my finale, I introduced myself and asked for his name in return. The personal introduction was the icing on the cake and with impeccable timing the doors opened to my floor. Though the conversation didn't last long, I had made a new friend, Lance, who worked in the company upstairs. The result of my bravery wasn't groundbreaking, but I noticed that starting my morning achieving a goal and having a pleasant conversation helped set a positive tone for the rest of the day. By the end of the week I had completed my daily elevator challenge with a strong sense of satisfaction and further proved to myself I had nothing to be afraid of.

Once I got this down, I applied it everywhere and started meeting new people left and right. Aside from hearing tons of interesting stories, stepping outside of my comfort zone started to make me shine brighter. I already had a warm personality, but this added ingredient of being able to fearlessly spark a conversation set me up to be the person who actually changed a room when I entered it; I started making a difference everywhere I went. I've heard you get what you put out in the world, and this experiment proved to me just that. As I was reaching out more often, I noticed that people were also reaching out to me. The energy was amplified—the more people I connected with, the more invites came my way. Opportunities were showing up all over the place. It felt like I had a seat at the table of life. It was clear that my life got better as soon as I started taking action. Because of this, I felt a strong sense of control over my destiny, which was incredibly empowering. With this awareness, my risk-taking enterprise took off. I took a quick inventory of what really scared me and decided to tackle these head on. I thought about all the areas in which I was holding myself back because of a deep-rooted fear. I had put off asking for a raise from my boss, and I secretly wanted to profess my interest for my latest crush. I vowed to tackle these next.

The uncomfortable territory of going after what I wanted started to feel less scary. Though I wouldn't ever absolve my fear of being rejected, I recognized that rejection was never the end; it was the catalyst for the next step. I loved who I was becoming and it was exhilarating to take charge of my life by taking action. All the risks I took paid off somehow. Whether it was a small payoff like making somebody's day, or a large payoff like changing the direction of my life—each risk provided an opportunity to evolve into the best version of myself. I was living my single life well—more than well, I was on fire. I didn't have time to be lonely; I was too busy growing and becoming a better me. I was too busy blazing trails in my life. With this confidence, I was able to attain almost everything I wanted and it really was magic.

——— **LESSON** ———

Life happens outside of your comfort zone.

· · · · · · HOMEWORK · · · · · ·

1. IDENTIFY AREAS OF YOUR LIFE in which you want to improve. Clearly define in 1 - 2 short sentences what it is you want out of each portion. Now break down some steps that could be a catalyst for movement in these areas of your life. Uses these steps to formulate a plan; treat your life like you would treat a business. Design everything just as you want it and then start to execute your plan.

2. IDENTIFY SITUATIONS that make your heart flutter with anxiety or anticipation. Enlist a friend's help and challenge yourself to take this situation head on. Do one a week. And use your friend for support when you want to chicken out.

3. ACKNOWLEDGE THE RISKS you've taken in your life. Write them down and then write what the results were. Were they positive, negative. Did you succeed or fail? What did you learn from each situation? If you had to do it over, would you do it differently? If so, why not recreate the situation and try again?

—— Appendix ——

SINGLE LIFE TOOLKIT

B ecause this book was written with the intent of helping singles live a single life they love, we wanted to add some additional tools to help during some tough single situations. Think of it like a quick start manual, when you need a boost.

—— Appendix A ——

THE AWESOME LIST

T he biggest discovery one can make while being single is learning that confidence not only comes from within, but also can be learned and practiced. One day we were sitting around venting about our latest dating woes. One of us would console the other and reply to the tale of rejection with a supportive girlfriend response like, "He doesn't know what he's missing, you're so awesome!"

This conversation naturally evolved into how unbelievable it was that we were both still single—we were good catches! We exceeded average in a lot of categories and were actually really awesome people in general. One by one we started shouting out qualities that made us awesome. The list grew as things like, "Yeah, and both of our hair goes curly and straight without much effort," and "We totally know how to dance and can do fierce high kicks," piled on.

Our ten minutes of enthusiastic praise escalated, and once we reached a stopping point, we both felt surprisingly re-freshed.

What started as venting and frustration about why things weren't turning out as desired ended up as an unbelievably effective ego boost. Through the process of making a list, we were reminded how amazing we truly were.

This exercise was so successful that day that we started to implement it anytime one of us felt dejected or frustrat-ed with our dating lives. Sometimes we implemented the list it for no reason other than to remember that we were awesome and we should be happy about it.

We encourage everybody to make an awesome list right now. Don't feel silly or self conscious at what goes on the list—just start. Every so often revisit the list and add to it.

To get you started, we included our very first awesome list (yes, we wrote it down) so that you get an idea of just how broad this list can be.

THE "WHY WE ARE AWESOME" LIST:

1. Funny
2. Smart
3. Like to read
4. Nice
5. We have awesome hair that goes both curly and straight
6. We have great shoes
7. We are fabulous dancers
8. Pretty
9. Sexy
10. Silly
11. Thoughtful
12. We can pick great wine just by looking at the label
13. We can rock the sweat pants and not worry about looking bad
14. We work out...hard!
15. Enjoy baths

16. We can laugh at ourselves harder than anybody else can laugh at us

17. We know what we want and don't feel bad about expecting it or asking for it

——— APPENDIX B ———

WHAT TO DO WHEN YOU'VE GOT NOTHING TO DO

B oredom and loneliness can sometimes feel like the punishment for being single. Sometimes curling up in sweatpants feels just fine, but when actually sitting on the sofa all alone, you might find yourself feeling down about your current life situation. The last thing you want to do is start texting your ex when you start to yearn for fulfillment. Rather than open up old wounds, pick something from the list below and feel better about all the time you have to yourself.

1. **PAMPER YOURSELF**: Paint your nails, put on a facial mask, take a bath with wine and great music, deep condition your hair. Time is a luxury; realize how rich you are

and use that time on things that make you feel better.

2. CATCH UP ON SLEEP: Seriously. As uneventful sleep is, almost all of us are sleep deprived and would enjoy our lives more if we aren't dragging ourselves around all day. Plus there's no better cure for tired skin and under eye circles than beauty rest.

3. BAKE A DELICIOUS TREAT: Challenge and reward in about 60 minutes or less. Also, if you don't want to eat the entire thing yourself, you can share with someone who could use a pick me up.

4. MAKE A LIST OF THINGS you hope to do/learn in your life and get started on one: Always wanted to learn a language? Because you're alone you won't feel silly attempting to pronounce foreign words for the first time.

5. GO FOR A WALK: It feels good to get out of the house. Take funny/interesting pictures along the way. Celebrate your surroundings.

6. CLEAN: Get it together and make your home a place where you feel your absolute best. When your surroundings are clean and organized, you'll feel accomplished

and ready to take on the world. A great way to get in the mood for some serious cleaning is to blast your favorite 90's Whitney Houston playlist and get moving.

7. TRY ON OUTFITS to pre-plan for the next time you feel like going out: Gather inspiration from magazines and web sites. Get creative with what you have in your closet. This will save the last minute panic next time you get an impromptu invite.

8. TAKE UP A HOBBY: Playing the guitar, Photoshop and learning how to buy and trade stocks are just a few ideas. Hobbies not only occupy our time, they make for more interesting and well-rounded people. Plus you never know where it could lead; we started this book one Saturday night when we didn't have anything else to do.

9. GO THROUGH YOUR CONTACTS and call every person you haven't talked to in a while and catch up: Reconnecting is a great mood booster and will also keep relationships and opportunities alive.

10. MAKE UN-CHRISTMAS CARDS: No matter what time of year it is, write, address, stamp and mail a batch

of cards. It will be a fun surprise for the receiver.

11. STRETCH: Your body will thank you for it.

······ **WHAT NOT TO DO** ······

1. CALL YOURSELF A LOSER for staying home. There's nothing wrong with enjoying your own company and taking care of yourself.

2. CALL/EMAIL/TEXT OLD BOYFRIENDS.

STEPH **YOUNG** & JILL **DICKMAN**

··· ACKNOWLEDGEMENTS ···

'd like to thank a few people. First and foremost, thank you to my parents, who gave me a wholesome childhood and instilled in me the belief that I could do anything. Thank you for providing unconditional love and support in all my adventures. To Roslyn Barnfield, you are truly my plus one and my better half. To my sisters, who have taught me so much. Team 113 for always keeping the fire under me. To Nils Parker, our editor, for being honest in your feedback and for your continued encouragement. To my friends who were patient with me when I locked myself in my apartment for a year to finish this book. And to everybody who supported in one way or another, every little notion, message and nudge contributed to this book finally being completed.

-STEPH YOUNG

would like to give thanks to my amazing parents who gave me a happy and stable childhood. And for always encouraging me to think for myself and follow my dreams. I'd like to thank my friends who pushed me, accepted me, and became family. And finally to all the boys over the years that helped me realize what love is, what love isn't, and how kickass it is to be me, regardless of relationship status.

- JILL DICKMAN

···· ABOUT THE AUTHORS ····

STEPH YOUNG AND JILL DICKMAN have been friends forever. Like any best friends, they spent countless hours sharing the stories of their unbelievable dating experiences, while seeking insight from each other about the bigger issues they faced. They soon realized there was a common theme through everything they had experienced. In fact, a lot of single women probably faced the same challenges. And since they were sharing these stories with each other already, they figured, "Why not share them, and the lessons we took from them, with the world?" And so here they are.

Steph works in marketing and lives in Los Angeles. Jill is a Bar Method and dance instructor in Portland, Oregon. They are both single, and loving it.